D0908539

SUICIDE AND HOMICIDE IN THE TWENTIETH CENTURY: CHANGES OVER TIME

SUICIDE AND HOMICIDE IN THE TWENTIETH CENTURY: CHANGES OVER TIME

DAVID LESTER AND BIJOU YANG

Nova Science Publishers, Inc.
Commack, New York

Editorial Production: Susan Boriotti
Office Manager: Annette Hellinger
Graphics: Frank Grucci and John T'Lustachowski
Information Editor: Tatiana Shohov
Book Production: Donna Dennis, Patrick Davin, Christine Mathosian, Tammy Sauter and Diane Sharp
Circulation: Maryanne Schmidt
Marketing/Sales: Cathy DeGregory

Library of Congress Cataloging-in-Publication Data

Lester, David, 1942- , and Yang, Bijou
    Suicide and homicide in the twentieth century : changes over time / David Lester and Bijou Yang.
          p.   cm.
    ISBN 1-56072-606-7
    1. Suicide--Research--Statistical methods. 2. Homicide--Research--Statistical methods. 3. Time-series analysis. I. Title.
HV6545.L4198   1998   98-35923
364.15'2'0904—dc21   CIP

Copyright © 1998 by Nova Science Publishers, Inc.
    6080 Jericho Turnpike, Suite 207
    Commack, New York 11725
    Tele. 516-499-3103   Fax 516-499-3146
    e-mail: Novascience@earthlink.net
    e-mail: Novascil@aol.com
    Web Site: http://www.nexusworld.com/nova

Printed in the United States of America

CONTENTS

Chapter One

INTRODUCTION

Lester (1996) conducted a cross-sectional (regional or ecological) study of the correlates of suicide and homicide rates in nations of the world in 1980. He concluded that there was good evidence that official statistics from the nations of the world were sufficiently reliable and valid so that cross-sectional research was meaningful. He found that the social correlates of suicide were opposite to those for homicide, supporting the theory of suicide and homicide proposed by Henry and Short (1954), who had argued that murderers and suicides experience different kinds of restraints on their behavior (external versus internal, respectively) and come from different social classes (lower versus higher, respectively) (Lester, 1989). The correlational analysis also revealed that suicide rates were positively associated with an index of urban and wealth, while homicide rates were negatively associated with this index.

It has been commonly noted that the results of correlational studies of societal suicide rates differ depending on whether time-series or regional studies are conducted. Sometimes, an hypothesis derived from sociological theory is confirmed in one type of study and not confirmed in the other type of study. This raises the possibility that different sociological theories may be required to explain the time-series suicide and homicide rates from those used to explain regional differences in suicide and homicide rates. This book explores the social correlates of suicide and homicide rates within nations over time, in contrast to Lester's (1996) book, which explored the social correlates over nations at one point in time (namely 1980).

AN EXAMPLE

There are some social indicators which show similar associations with suicide rates in both time-series and regional studies. For example, the Pearson correlation between the divorce rate and the suicide rate over the 48 continental contiguous states of America in 1980 was 0.78 (two-tailed $p <$ .001) (Lester, 1994). Over time in the United States, from 1945 to 1984, the Pearson correlation was 0.60 ($p < $.001). Regression analyses confirmed these results.

However, there are social indicators which give different results in the two types of studies: in Lester's (1994) study of the United States, unemployment was correlated with suicide rates over time ($r = 0.76$) but not over the states ($r = -0.11$). Using regression analyses (Yang, 1989, 1992; Yang and Lester, 1997), a similar result was found in a time-series analysis of the United States and a cross-sectional study of the 48 continental contiguous states in 1980. Unemployment was a significant variable in the regression model for suicide rates over time but not over states.

STATISTICAL ISSUES

PROBLEMS IN REGRESSION ANALYSES

Regional studies which have used regression analyses have hitherto typically ignored the problem of spatial autocorrelation (Odland, 1988). In general, this refers to the fact that a sample of regions is not generally a sample of *independent* subjects as required by a random sampling process, but rather are spatially related. Neighboring regions resemble one another in social characteristics owing to geographic proximity. For example, suicide rates increase rather regularly from the eastern states to the western states in

America.[1]

Time-series studies, similarly, must take into account simple monotonic time trends in their data which can be taken into account by including "year" as one of the variables in the regression analysis or by examining deviations from linear regression trends in the social indicators rather than their absolute values. However, time-series regression analyses have to consider a much greater variety of other statistical problems (including serial autocorrelation [Greene, 1990]), problems which introduce a great deal of choice in the particular type of time-series regression technique.

FREEZING TIME AND PLACE

Regional studies typically take one year and examine the regional associations between social characteristics in that year. It may, therefore, be more useful to replicate a regional study in several years, so that its generality can be examined. No study of this type has been conducted on suicide, but Bailey (1980) carried out cross-sectional analyses of the effect of executions on homicide rates over the states of America for each of 29 different years. Twenty years gave a deterrent effect (executions reduce the murder rate), seven a brutalization effect (executions increase the murder rate), and one a zero effect. It can be seen that the replications permit an examination of the reliability of a result.

Correspondingly, time-series analyses typically chose one region for which to examine the associations between social characteristics over time. It may be more useful to replicate time-series analyses in several regions so that their generality can be examined. For example, Yang and Lester (1994) examined the association between unemployment and suicide from 1950 to 1985 in twelve nations, finding the association in four and failing to find it in eight.

There are some investigators who combine both types of data. For example, data on the 48 contiguous states could be examined in ten different

---

[1] Although including latitude and longitude as variables in the regression analyses can take into account simple monotonic trends, spatial autocorrelation includes more complicated spatial variations

years, and the 480 data points examined together in one data analysis. For example, Trovato and Vos (1990) examined the impact of three social indicators (religious affiliation, married female labor force participation and divorce) as well as time period (1970-72 and 1980-82) on the suicide rates of the Canadian provinces, and found that domestic and religious individualism was positively related to suicide in both 15-19 year olds and 20-29 year olds and that the time period also had a significant effect.

EXPLAINING THE DIFFERENCES IN RESULTS

STABILITY VERSUS CHANGE

Regional studies tend to examine stable patterns in social characteristics, characteristics which may be closely related to geographic proximity. Social indicators do not typically change dramatically from year to year. For example, western states in the United States tend to have higher suicide rates than eastern states year after year, a finding which might be a result of differences in the regional culture and in the attitudes of the residents of western and eastern states. In contrast, time-series studies are examining variables which, though they may sometimes change only a little, do *change*. Thus, time-series analyses may be more sensitive to these variations from year to year and to those variables that take some time to change.

THE COMPARISONS MADE BY PEOPLE

If we consider the association between unemployment and suicide at the micro level, we would focus on how the economy acts as a suicidogenic stressor on the individual. For economic issues, do people compare their financial situation with their situation in previous years or with the situation of individuals in different regions? For some variables, the comparison may be with people in other regions, while for other variables people may monitor their own situation over time.

It is likely that a cross-sectional study will pick up situations where people compare themselves with those in other regions, whereas a time-series study showcases the situation where people compare their current situation with their situation in the past. This difference may explain, in part, why unemployment is a significant factor in time-series analyses but not in cross-sectional analyses. Changing unemployment rates in one region have an immediate impact on people in that region, regardless of what is happening in other regions.

Related to this is the tendency of people to adjust to situations over time. If an event happens relatively suddenly, such as a high unemployment rate, then people react because the event affects their immediate expectations. However, if the situation persists for a long period of time, then people tend to adjust to it. Cross-sectional analyses may pick up short-term effects whereas the influence of these short-term effects will be minimized in time-series analyses.

MEDIATING FACTORS

Variables may also differ in the timing of their impact on people and in whether they act directly or manifest their impact through other variables. For example, if a person is laid off or fired from their job, they may become depressed as a result. If the person remains unemployed, the person's marriage may be subjected to additional stress, and divorce may become more likely. The divorce may devastate the individual and lead to suicidal behavior. Thus, the link between divorce and suicidal behavior may be more immediate in time than the link between unemployment and suicidal behavior. As a result, the impact of divorce may show up in cross-sectional studies whereas the impact on unemployment may not.

PLAN OF THE BOOK

This book will present the results of time-series analyses of suicide and homicide rates within nations. What predicts the changes in these rates, and are these predictors different from those of cross-sectional studies? It complements, therefore, the earlier volume (Lester, 1996) which presented data comparing suicide and homicide in different nations in one time period -- 1980.

Collecting time-series data is quite difficult, for many nations have never prepared such data sets. Furthermore, several nations have missing data for some years in a given time-series. The present book is based on four major data sets.

First, suicide and homicide rates were collected for the total population and for men and women separately for the period 1950-1985. Second, suicide rates by gender and by age were collected for a smaller set of nations for the period 1960-1990. Third, suicide rates were collected for the period 1901-1988, total and by gender, and finally, suicide rates were located for longer periods of time for some nations, such as Finland (1751-1988) and for Switzerland (1876-1988).

REFERENCES

Bailey, W. A multivariate cross-sectional analysis of the deterrent effect of the death penalty. *Sociology & Social Research*, 1980, 64, 183-207.

Greene, W. H. *Econometric analysis*. New York: Macmillan, 1990.

Henry, A. F., & Short, J. F. *Suicide and homicide*. New York: Free Press, 1954.

Lester, D. *Suicide from a sociological perspective*. Springfield, IL: Charles Thomas, 1989.

Lester, D. Patterns *of suicide and homicide in America*. Commack, NY: Nova Science, 1994.

Lester, D. *Patterns of suicide and homicide in the world*. Commack, NY: Nova Science, 1996.

Lester, D., & Yang, B. *The economy and suicide*. Commack, NY: Nova Science, 1997.

Odland, J. *Spatial autocorrelation*. Beverly Hills, CA: Sage, 1988.

Trovato, F., & Vos, R. Domestic/religious individualism and youth suicide in Canada. *Family Perspective*, 1990, 24(1), 69-81.

Yang, B. A real income hypothesis of suicide: A cross-sectional study of the United States. Eastern Economic Association, Baltimore, 1989.

Yang, B. The economy and suicide. *American Journal of Economics & Sociology*, 1992, 51, 87-99.

Yang, B., & Lester, D. The social impact of unemployment. *Applied Economics Letters*, 1994, 1, 223-226

Chapter Two

TIME-SERIES ANALYSES, 1950-1985

The present chapter explores the variation in suicide and homicide rates over time within nations. Two major sets of predictors are explored. First, in Durkheim's (1897) theory of suicide, social integration and social regulation are the two determinants of the suicide rate. A society is integrated insofar as its members possess durable and stable social relationships (Gibbs and Martin, 1964), and it is regulated insofar as the emotions and motivations of its members are controlled by societal norms and customs. The measures of domestic social integration used here to predict the time-series suicide and homicide rates were marriage, birth and divorce rates.

Previous research on this issue has studied only one or two nations, and used different time periods, different measures of divorce and other variables, different statistical packages and different sets of variables in the multiple regression analyses. For example, Yang, et al. (1992) used the divorce rate, Lester and Yang (1991) used the ratio of divorces to marriages, while Stack (1990) used the number of divorces divided by the numbers of divorces plus marriages.

It would be of great interest to use uniform time periods, sets of variables, and statistical techniques to examine the reliability of the associations between suicide rates and domestic integration over time in nations. The present study was designed to do this for a set of nations with available data.

METHOD

Data on suicide and homicide rates from 1950 to 1985 were obtained from the World Health Organization (annual). However, some of the nations in the sample had missing data for one or more years. The authors obtained data for the missing years by writing to suicidologists in those nations to obtain xeroxed copies of official government tables of suicide and homicide rates. The suicide and homicide rates are shown in Appendix A.

Choice of the independent variables was limited by the difficulty of obtaining 35 years of continuous data. Few nations can provide such long-term time-series data on social indicators. The three measures of domestic integration used were the crude marriage, divorce and birth rates, obtained from the United Nations (annual). This data set was used since it is easily obtainable by other investigators wishing to replicate the present study and because the use of a single data source ensures some standardization of the data.

The time-series regressions were carried using a statistical package from Doan (1990), with the Cochrane-Orcutt method to correct for serial autocorrelation which was present in many of the national data sets.

RESULTS

SUICIDE AND DOMESTIC INTEGRATION

The results of the time-series regressions are shown in Table 2.1. It can be seen that the majority of the regression coefficients for the marriage rate were negative (20 out of 29, $X^2 = 4.17$, df = 1, p < .05), indicating that higher marriage rates are typically associated with lower suicide rates as predicted by Durkheim. Six of these regression coefficients were negative and statistically significant while none was positive and statistically significant (one-tailed binomial p = .016), confirming the above conclusion.

For divorce rates, 22 of the regression coefficients were positive and 7 were negative ($X^2 = 7.76$, df = 1, p < .01), indicating that higher divorce rates are typically associated with higher suicide rates as predicted by Durkheim. Twelve of the positive regression coefficients were statistically significant while only one of the negative coefficients was statistically significant (one-tailed binomial p = .004).

For the birth rate, however, 12 of the regression coefficients were positive (6 significantly so) and 17 were negative (4 significantly so), indicating no significant trend toward a positive or a negative association.

Since the signs for the associations in the sample of 29 nations were sometimes positive and sometimes negative, it was decided to examine whether the social indicators used in the analyses could predict the signs of the association. This was done by calculating point-biserial correlation coefficients between the sign of the regression coefficients (negative coded as zero and positive coded as one) and the suicide, marriage, birth and divorce rates of the nations in 1950 and, in addition, the real gross domestic product per capita in 1950 obtained from Summers and Heston (1984) using a slightly smaller sample of 27 nations (Lester, 1997).

None of these variables was associated with the sign of the regression coefficients for marriage or divorce rates. However, the sign of the regression coefficient for birth rates was negatively associated with 1950 marriage rates (r = -0.47, two-tailed p = .012). Nations with a negative regression coefficient for birth rates (as predicted by Durkheim's theory) had significantly higher marriage rates in 1950 than nations with a positive regression coefficient. Thus, Durkheim's theory as it pertains to societal birth rates was supported in nations where the marriage rate was high, but it was not supported in societies when the marriage rate was low.

SUICIDE, MARRIAGE AND BIRTH RATES

Several nations either do not report divorce rates consistently or do not permit divorce, and so divorce rates are unavailable. The analyses were run, therefore, just for marriage and birth rates so that these nations could be included.

The results of the regression analyses of the time-series data sets are shown in Table 2.2. For marriage rates, it can be seen that, the regression coefficient was negative for 22 of the 36 nations (X^2 = 1.78, df = 1, ns). Of those statistically significant, however, seven out of seven were negative (binomial p = .008). Thus, there is a clear-cut trend for nations with a higher the marriage rate to have a lower suicide rate.

For birth rates, the regression coefficient was negative for 24 of the 36 nations (X^2 = 4.00, df = 1, p < .05). Of those statistically significant, nine were negative and four positive (binomial p = .13). Clearly the effect of the birth rate on the suicide rate was weaker than the effect of the marriage rate.

The multiple R^2 values ranged from 0.03 for Liechtenstein and Singapore to 0.97 for Canada and Sri Lanka, with a median value of 0.79, indicating that, in general, these two predictor variables (the marriage and birth rates) were quite successful in predicting the suicide rate.

MULTICOLLINEARITY

To explore the effect of multicollinearity in the independent variables, the Pearson correlations between each of the independent and dependent variables are shown in Table 2.3, and the results of simple linear time-series regressions for the suicide rate on each independent variable are shown in Table 2.4.

It can be seen in Table 2.3 that marriage and birth rates, marriage and divorce rates and birth and divorce rates were consistently associated in the sample of nations. Interestingly, however, some deviations appeared. In the United States, the correlation between marriage and birth rates was negative, not positive, and the correlation between marriage and divorce rates positive, not negative, possibly due to the high rate of remarriage in the United States.

The Pearson correlations indicated negative correlations between both the marriage and birth rates and the suicide rate and a positive correlation between the divorce rate and the suicide rate. Again, there were exceptions to this (for example, in Australia and England/Wales), and not all of the associations were statistically significant.

The results of the bivariate regressions of the suicide rate on each independent variable alone are shown in Table 2.4. It can be seen that the marriage rate and the suicide rate were significantly associated in only six of the 36 nations, whereas the positive association between the divorce rate and the suicide rate was statistically significant and positive in 15 nations and negative in one nation. The birth rate and the suicide rate were significantly associated negatively in 12 nations and positively in three nations. Thus, both birth and divorce rates appear to be more strongly associated with the suicide rate than marriage rates.

HOMICIDE AND DOMESTIC INTEGRATION

The results for homicide for 19 nations are shown in Table 2.5. For divorce rates, it can be seen that 15 of the regression coefficients were positive and four negative (two-tailed binomial p = 0.02). The data for Hungary for 1956 include those killed in the 1956 revolution. Using interpolation for the homicide rate for 1956[2], 16 of the regression coefficients were now positive and three negative (two-tailed binomial p = 0.004). All eight of the regression coefficients reaching statistical significance were positive (two-tailed binomial p = 0.008).

The results for marriage and birth rates were not so clear-cut. For marriage rates, ten regression coefficients were positive and nine were negative, while for birth rates six regression coefficients were positive and 13 were negative. The results for just marriage and birth rates are shown in Table 2.6.

The general trend identified for time-series homicide rates is that homicide rates are positively associated with divorce rates. Thus, when divorce rates are higher, homicide rates are also higher. It was predicted from Henry and Short's theory that opposite associations would be found for homicide and suicide rates. This was not confirmed here, for divorce rates were positively associated with both homicide and suicide rates in this sample of nations. In addition, marriage rates were negatively associated with suicide rates but not associated with homicide rates. Thus, homicide and suicide rates did not show opposite associations as predicted by Henry and Short (1954).

---

[2] the average of the rates for 1955 and 1957.

DIVORCE/MARRIAGE RATIOS

As mentioned at the beginning of this chapter, some investigators have suggested using a ratio measure for divorce and marriage rates. To explore the effect of this tactic, the regressions were run for suicide first using the marriage and divorce rates separately in the regression analyses and then using the divorce/marriage rate ratio. The results are shown in Table 2.7, where it can be seen that the results are similar for both sets of analyses. Divorce rates were positively associated with suicide for 22 of the 29 nations, as was the divorce/marriage rate ratio. The R^2 values were similar for both sets of analyses, though the general tendency was for R^2 to be a little higher when marriage and divorce rates were used separately (eleven higher versus three lower). Thus, the use of the ratio measure does not appear to improve predictive accuracy.

DISCUSSION

The present study used uniform time-periods, data sets, variable definitions, and regression techniques to explore the validity of Durkheim's theory relating domestic integration to suicide in thirty-six nations. The results indicated good agreement with predictions for marriage and divorce rates, but poor agreement for birth rates. However, support for the predictions regarding marriage and divorce rates was not obtained in every nation studied.

Thus, this study shows the importance of cross-cultural replication of studies in order to provide some idea of the generality of the results reported. Studies of merely one or two nations are not sufficient to provide this information.

Once a study such as the present one has been conducted, research can then proceed to the next question, namely under what conditions are the predicted associations obtained? The present study provided some answers for the effect of birth rates on suicide. The predicted effect (a negative association as predicted by Durkheim) was found in nations with higher marriage rates. This enables us to speculate that, perhaps, the beneficial impact of children with respect to suicidal behavior is found only in nations with relatively higher marriage rates. This, of course, requires further research to explore the mechanisms by which this differential effect might be caused.

It should also be noted that suicide rates vary greatly within some nations and that not every region of the nation may show the same pattern. For example, in Canada, time-series analyses of the suicide rate in Quebec do not always produce the same results as similar analyses in other provinces (Cormier and Klerman, 1985). In the present study, separate analyses were run for the three regions in the United Kingdom (England/Wales, Scotland, and Northern Ireland) since the British government typically reports statistics for these three regions separately. Conducting separate analyses for the different regions in other nations may also be fruitful.

It is clear, therefore, that the results of the present study are stimulating for future research.

REFERENCES

Cormier, H. J., & Klerman, G. L. Unemployment and male-female labor force participation as determinants of changing suicide rates of males and females in Quebec. *Social Psychiatry*, 1985, 20, 109-114.

Doan, T. A. *Regression analysis of time series*. Evanston, IL: Var Econometrics, 1990.

Durkheim, E. *Le suicide*. Paris: Felix Alcan, 1897.

Gibbs, J. P., & Martin, W. T. *Status integration and suicide*. Eugene, OR: University of Oregon, 1964.

Henry, A. F., & Short, J. F. *Suicide and homicide*, New York: Free Press, 1954.

Lester, D. *Suicide and homicide around the world*. Commack, NY: Nova Science, 1997.

Lester, D., & Yang, B. The relationship between divorce, unemployment and female participation in the labour force and suicide rates in Australia and America. *Australian & New Zealand Journal of Psychiatry*, 1991, 25, 519-523.

Stack, S. The effect of divorce on suicide in Denmark, 1951-1980. *Sociological Quarterly*, 1990, 31, 359-370.

Summers, R., & Heston, A. Improved international comparisons of real product and its composition. *Review of Income Wealth*, 1984, 30, 207-262.

United Nations. *Demographic Yearbook.* New York: United Nations, annual.

World Health Organization. *Statistics Annual.* Geneva, Switzerland: World Health Organization, annual.

Yang, B., Lester, D., & Yang, C. H. Sociological and economic theories of suicide. *Social Science & Medicine*, 1992, 34, 333-334.

Table 2.1
Results Of The Multiple Time-Series Regressions Of The Suicide Rate For 29
Nations

	constant	Marriage rate	Birth rate	Divorce rate	R^2	Durbin-Watson statistic
Australia	8.928	0.004	0.189	-0.181	0.69	1.78
Austria	11.787**	-0.150	0.219	6.967***	0.81	20.3
Belgium	19.050	-0.869	-0.076	5.476*	0.95	1.89
Canada	10.796***	0.130	-0.192***	1.961***	0.98	1.56
Costa Rica	4.312***	0.050	-0.047*	1.495	0.63	2.03
Czechoslov.	28.449***	0.382	-0.327	-2.649	0.79	2.36
Denmark	23.383	-0.251	-0.363	3.410	0.84	2.01
England/Wales	8.434**	-0.653	0.390	-0.043	0.95	1.30
Finland	19.639	-0.137	-0.075	3.487*	0.86	2.16
France	12.078**	-1.068**	0.437*	4.872***	0.95	2.28
Hungary	49.455**	-0.550	-0.213	3.204	0.96	2.45
Iceland	27.981	-0.355	-0.469	-2.904	0.20	1.71
Japan	3.126	0.590	-0.249	10.292*	0.86	1.11
Luxembourg#	21.666**	-1.113	-0.284	3.651	0.69	1.90
Mauritius	1.060	0.033	-0.014	16.033*	0.45	2.03
Mexico	1.418	-0.084	0.018	-0.121	0.27	2.01
Netherlands	5.286	0.036	-0.021	2.712***	0.96	1.62
New Zealand	11.322***	-0.282	-0.010	0.632	0.49	1.97
N. Ireland	-1.602	0.352	0.373*	4.721***	0.65	2.13
Norway	0.242	-0.738**	0.462	6.323***	0.96	1.93
Portugal##	8.424***	-0.217	0.100	1.134	0.34	2.02
Puerto Rico	2.104	-0.078	0.273*	0.407	0.65	2.06
Scotland	6.653	-0.051	0.083	1.008	0.83	1.98
Sweden	12.078*	-1.076	0.968*	0.337	0.58	2.03
Switzerland	15.412	0.924	-0.488	5.357	0.90	2.06
Taiwan	2.040	0.205	0.266*	2.649	0.80	2.10
USA	16.310***	-0.368***	-0.151***	0.430***	0.92	2.08
West Germany	26.757***	-0.754*	-0.038	-0.359	0.80	1.87
Yugoslavia	32.110***	-1.175***	-0.242***	-3.701***	0.93	1.28
Positive		9	12	22		

David Lester and Bijou Yang

		20	17	7		
Negative		20	17	7		
Significant & positive		0	6	12		
Significant & negative		6	4	1		

\# interpolation used for one year of missing suicide rates
\#\# interpolation used for three years of missing suicide rates

*** p < .001
** p < .01
*   p < .05

Table 2.2
Results Of The Multiple Regression Analyses For The Suicide Rate On
Marriage And Birth Rates For 36 Nations
(b coefficients are shown)

	constant	marriage rate	birth rate	R^2	Durbin-Watson Statistic
Australia	8.19	-0.09	0.25	0.69	1.78
Austria	29.24***	0.02	-0.36	0.69	2.19
Belgium	45.52***	-2.05*	-0.97***	0.94	1.71
Canada	16.39**	0.04	-0.24	0.97	1.45
Chile#	7.78*	-0.25	0.01	0.36	1.49
Costa Rica	3.49*	0.35	-0.07*	0.56	2.05
Czechoslov.	25.00***	0.18	-0.33	0.77	2.39
Denmark	40.92***	-1.53	-0.47	0.82	2.07
England/ Wales	8.29**	-0.66*	0.39**	0.95	1.31
Finland	35.99***	-0.67	-0.55	0.83	1.97
France	151.38*	-0.91	0.39	0.93	2.41
Hungary	70.47**	0.14	-0.46	0.96	2.48
Iceland	15.62*	-0.06	-0.19	0.18	1.68
Ireland	14.42*	0.12	-0.36	0.89	2.42
Italy	10.41	-0.51	-0.04	0.59	2.00
Japan	18.17**	0.36	-0.20	0.84	1.20
Liechtenstein	24.36	-0.31	-0.51	0.03	1.91
Luxembourg#	35.60***	-2.11*	-0.61	0.67	1.95
Mauritius	2.14	0.40	-0.01	0.36	1.95
Mexico	1.36	-0.08	0.02	0.27	2.02
Netherlands	17.11***	-0.39	-0.34***	0.94	1.50
New Zealand	15.05***	-0.34	-0.12**	0.43	2.04
N. Ireland	9.34	-0.90	0.11	0.57	2.20
Norway	25.83***	-0.96	-0.64**	0.94	1.99
Portugal###	10.30***	-0.21	0.02	0.32	2.02

Puerto Rico	4.18	0.02	0.21***	0.64	2.07
Scotland	8.64	0.36	0.13	0.83	2.07
Singapore	8.76*	0.12	0.01	0.03	1.80
Spain##	8.00***	-0.23	-0.08	0.88	1.11
Sri Lanka	353.08	0.57	-0.60	0.97	1.68
Sweden	13.73***	-1.11*	0.90*	0.58	2.05
Switzerland	31.59***	0.69	-1.02**	0.89	1.95
Taiwan	4.11	0.22	0.24*	0.79	2.05
USA	19.58***	-0.32	-0.27***	0.90	1.89
West Germany	25.81***	-0.73*	-0.01	0.79	1.85
Yugoslavia	27.50***	-1.11***	-0.24***	0.89	1.54

\#   interpolation used for one year of missing suicide rates
\#\#   interpolation used for two years of missing suicide rates
\#\#\# interpolation used for three years of missing suicide rates

*   p < .05
**   p < .01
*** p < .001

Table 2.3
Pearson Correlations Between The Suicide Rate And Measures Of Domestic
Integration

	Marriage & birth	Marriage & divorce	Divorce & birth	Suicide & marriage	Suicide & birth	Suicide & divorce
Australia	0.37	-0.39*	-0.87*	0.04	0.04	-0.30
Austria	0.79*	-0.62*	-0.83*	-0.55*	-0.65*	0.87*
Belgium	0.53*	-0.73*	-0.92*	-0.78*	-0.84*	0.95
Canada	-0.07	0.01	-0.86*	0.06	-0.93*	0.97*
Chile	0.20	-	-	-0.17	-0.01	-
Costa Rica	-0.36*	0.69*	-0.58*	0.49*	-0.68*	0.72*
Czechoslovakia	0.55*	0.10	-0.42*	0.17	-0.41*	0.12
Denmark	0.93*	-0.93*	-0.90*	-0.81*	-0.77*	0.81*
England/Wales	0.43*	-0.49*	-0.87*	-0.01	0.74*	-0.80*
Finland	0.46*	-0.65*	-0.85*	-0.63*	-0.87*	0.85*
France	0.59*	-0.77*	-0.83*	-0.90*	-0.63*	0.89*
Hungary	0.83*	-0.65*	-0.66*	-0.68*	-0.58*	0.94*
Iceland	0.62*	-0.70*	-0.92*	-0.15	-0.21	0.14
Ireland	0.46*	-	-	-0.02	-0.66*	-
Italy	0.95*	-	-	-0.65*	-0.60*	-
Japan	0.47*	-0.78*	-0.54*	-0.31	0.05	-0.07
Liechtenstein	-0.56*	-	-	-0.01	-0.14	-
Luxembourg	0.65*	-0.77*	-0.80*	-0.68*	-0.71*	0.80*
Mauritius	-0.59*	0.60*	-0.28	0.37*	0.02	0.47*
Mexico	-0.09	-0.24	0.30	-0.22	0.45*	0.05
Netherlands	0.75*	-0.86*	-0.94*	-0.82*	-0.94*	0.97*
New Zealand	0.41*	-0.41*	-0.88*	-0.42*	-0.62*	0.68*
N. Ireland	0.48*	-0.39*	-0.72*	-0.13	-0.18	0.66
Norway	0.88*	-0.82*	-0.98*	-0.86*	-0.95*	0.97*
Portugal	0.17	-0.25	-0.85*	-0.42*	0.16	0.04
Puerto Rico	-0.61*	0.74*	-0.93*	-0.44*	0.78*	-0.69*
Scotland	0.67*	-0.78*	-0.92*	-0.68*	-0.51*	0.71*
Singapore	-0.95*	-	-	0.02	-0.01	-

Spain	0.91*	-	-	-0.13	-0.15	-
Sweden	0.91*	-0.83*	-0.80*	-0.35*	-0.20	0.27
Switzerland	0.95*	-0.93*	-0.96*	-0.63*	-0.75*	0.77*
Taiwan	0.03	0.42*	-0.45*	-0.41*	0.63*	-0.35*
USA	-0.63*	0.66*	-0.88*	0.56*	-0.90*	0.90
West Germany	0.89*	-0.63*	-0.74*	-0.86*	-0.77*	0.52*
Yugoslavia	0.88*	-0.13	-0.15	-0.88*	-0.91*	-0.03

* two-tailed p = .05 or better

Table 2.4
Results Of the Linear Regressions For the Suicide Rate On Measures Of
Domestic Integration Alone
(b coefficients shown, correcting for serial autocorrelation)

	marriage	birth	divorce
Australia	0.115	0.241	-0.307
Austria	0.106	-0.357	5.633***
Belgium	-0.420	-0.209	6.514***
Canada	0.382	-0.252	1.743***
Chile	-0.254	-0.058	-
Costa Rica	0.469	-0.081***	2.247***
Czechoslovakia	0.129	-0.314	-2.390
Denmark	-2.422***	-0.989***	4.829***
England/Wales	-0.573	0.358*	-0.542
Finland	-0.222	-0.522*	3.946***
France	-0.709	0.276	4.810***
Hungary	-0.033	-0.442	2.759
Iceland	-0.442	-0.198	0.712
Ireland	-0.082	-0.335	-
Italy	-0.629**	-0.193**	-
Japan	0.162	-0.176	8.389
Liechtenstein	0.001	-0.362	-
Luxembourg	-3.028***	-1.236**	6.365***
Mauritius	0.404	-0.103	16.611*
Mexico	-0.063	0.017	0.110
Netherlands	-0.133	-0.416***	2.766***
New Zealand	-0.645	-0.141**	0.750***
Northern Ireland	-0.817	-0.014	2.988**
Norway	-0.973*	-0.987***	5.225***
Portugal	-0.173	-0.014	0.600
Puerto Rico	-0.207	0.210***	-0.822**
Scotland	0.311	0.110	0.803
Singapore	0.075	-0.021	-

Spain	-0.290	-0.119	-
Sri Lanka	0.183	-0.564	-
Sweden	-0.120	0.336	0.014
Switzerland	-0.764	-0.815***	6.768***
Taiwan	0.421	0.242**	1.176
USA	0.034	-0.218***	0.689***
West Germany	-0.763***	-0.257**	-0.276
Yugoslavia	-2.002***	-0.398***	-1.902

Table 2.5
Regression Coefficients For Time-Series Multiple Regressions Of The
Homicide Rates, 1950-1985

	constant	marriage	birth	divorce	R^2	Durbin-Watson
Australia	1.953*	0.013	-0.032	0.125*	0.79	1.94
Belgium	3.359	-0.188	-0.086	0.233	0.84	1.85
Canada	1.244	0.120	-0.041*	0.327*	0.94	2.26
England/Wales	-0.081	0.107	-0.016	0.109	0.67	2.14
Finland	-1.393	0.053	0.121*	1.178*	0.48	2.00
France	5.766	-0.441	-0.057	-0.756	0.06	2.01
Hungary	9.445	-1.212	0.511	-1.589	0.08	1.99
Hungary#	2.578	-0.096	0.082	0.894*	0.50	1.74
Iceland	-6.509*	0.297	0.121	1.830*	0.23	2.07
Japan+	-9.550*	0.028	-0.005	0.754	0.96	1.76
Netherlands	1.038*	0.010	-0.042*	0.137*	0.95	2.04
New Zealand	3.241*	-0.092	-0.061	-0.025	0.54	1.90
N. Ireland	58.191*	-2.524*	-1.755*	-5.510	0.86	1.94
Norway	0.402	-0.004	-0.004	0.352	0.73	1.91
Puerto Rico	-10.032	-4.186	1.393	10.017	0.03	2.02
Scotland	3.897	-0.279	-0.046	0.123	0.74	2.38
Sweden	0.729	-0.080	0.018	0.243*	0.81	2.00
USA	0.913	0.305	-0.051	1.245*	0.97	1.65
West Germany	1.279*	0.030	-0.029	0.183	0.68	2.26
Yugoslavia	-4.934*	0.738*	0.068	0.349	0.87	1.68

* significant at the 5% level or better
# recalculated using a homicide rate for 1956 which was the average of 1955
and 1957
+ interpolation used for one year of missing homicide rates

Table 2.6
Multiple Regression Results Of The Homicide Rates On The Marriage And
Birth Rates

	constant	marriage	birth	R^2	Durbin-Watson
Australia	2.998*	-0.005	-0.069*	0.74	1.90
Belgium	4.671*	-0.263*	-0.125*	0.83	1.83
Canada	2.883*	0.074	-0.082*	0.92	2.29
England/Wales	0.711	0.094	-0.050	0.66	2.26
Finland	4.382*	-0.193	-0.022	0.36	2.18
France	1.355	-0.112	0.030	0.60	1.69
Hungary	2.379	-0.960	0.606	0.07	2.00
Hungary#	3.181	-0.001	-0.391	0.38	2.02
Iceland	1.557	0.085	-0.059	0.06	1.97
Ireland	1.393	0.271*	-0.120	0.29	2.15
Japan+	0.419	0.040	-0.003	0.95	1.78
Netherlands	1.650*	-0.016	-0.058*	0.95	2.10
New Zealand	3.090	-0.090	-0.056*	0.54	1.90
N. Ireland	49.717*	-2.768*	-1.347*	0.85	1.88
Norway	1.811*	-0.008	-0.068	0.72	1.91
Puerto Rico	14.581	1.122*	-0.543*	0.87	1.52
Scotland	4.705*	-0.316	-0.070	0.74	2.40
Sweden	1.965*	-0.143*	0.013	0.71	2.09
USA	6.329	0.424	-0.094	0.97	1.32
Yugoslavia	-4.526*	0.737*	0.067	0.87	1.72

* significant at the .05 level or better
# recalculated using a homicide rate for 1956 which was the average of 1955 and 1957
+ interpolation used for one year of missing homicide rates

Table 2.7
Predicting Suicide Rates Using Marriage And Divorce Rates
(the regression coefficient for the constant is omitted from the table)

	marriage	divorce	R^2	divorce/ marriage	R^2
Australia	0.197	-0.319	0.68	-2.587	0.68
Austria	0.113	5.900*	0.80	21.806*	0.74
Belgium	-0.776	5.873*	0.95	38.050*	0.95
Canada	0.132	1.685*	0.97	15.394*	0.97
Costa Rica	0.018	2.214*	0.56	18.848*	0.57
Czechoslovakia	0.283	-2.649	0.78	-19.090	0.78
Denmark	-0.719	3.725*	0.83	20.717*	0.83
England/Wales	-0.483	-0.382	0.94	-3.460	0.93
Finland	-0.110	3.841*	0.86	20.621*	0.85
France	-1.034	3.351*	0.94	23.238*	0.94
Hungary	-0.703	3.592*	0.96	32.447*	0.96
Iceland	-0.378	0.220	0.17	4.970	0.17
Japan	0.348	8.588	0.85	11.769	0.84
Luxembourg	-1.257	4.358*	0.69	32.459*	0.66
Mauritius	0.061	15.890*	0.45	75.649	0.38
Mexico	-0.059	0.071	0.21	0.969	0.21
Netherlands	0.048	2.843*	0.96	14.205*	0.95
New Zealand	-0.286	0.673*	0.49	5.818*	0.49
N. Ireland	-0.406	2.727*	0.61	20.068*	0.61
Norway	-0.579*	4.260*	0.96	24.288*	0.97
Portugal	-0.132	0.359	0.32	1.323	0.31
Puerto Rico	0.045	-0.856*	0.57	-9.127*	0.56
Scotland	0.025	0.799	0.83	5.719	0.83
Sweden	-0.137	-0.068	0.52	0.271	0.52
Switzerland	0.437	73682*	0.89	26.716*	0.88
Taiwan	0.441	1.843	0.75	-4.059	0.75
USA	-0.247	0.807*	0.88	8.101*	0.88
West Germany	-0.833*	-0.319	0.80	-1.649	0.76
Yugoslavia	-2.162*	-3.237*	0.86	-15.276	0.90

* significant at the 5% level or better

Chapter Three

DOMESTIC INTEGRATION AND SUICIDE IN MEN AND WOMEN

Gove (1979) showed that marriage had a greater beneficial effect for men on their mental health in America as compared to women (using indices such as psychiatric disturbance and suicide), whereas being single had a greater beneficial effect for women on their mental health as compared to men.

More recently, a study of prefectures in Japan (Chandler and Tsai, 1993) indicated that the suicide rate of women was higher in those prefectures where marriage was more common and divorce less common, the opposite associations to those found for male suicide rates. Using Durkheim's (1897) typology of suicide, Chandler and Tsai suggested that, whereas the suicidal behavior of men may be anomic and egoistic in nature (that is, a result of too little social regulation and integration), the suicidal behavior of women may be fatalistic and altruistic in nature (that is, a result of too much social regulation and integration).

To explore this in time-series suicide rates, the present chapter explores whether measures of domestic integration are associated with the male and female suicide rates in a similar direction or in an opposite direction in 23 nations for the period 1950-1985 using, as before, the statistical package from

Doan (1990) and the Cochrane-Orcutt technique to correct for serial autocorrelation. The male and female suicide rates are shown in Appendix B.

The results are shown in Table 3.1. It can be seen that the association between marriage rates and suicide was negative for 18 of the 23 nations for men and for 13 of the 23 nations for women, a difference which failed to reach statistical significance. Among the significant coefficients, all six were negative for men, while three of out four were negative and one was positive for women. It seems that marriage rates have a somewhat stronger negative association with suicide for men than for women, though not significantly so.

For birth rates, ten of the associations were negative for men versus 16 for women. For the statistically significant coefficients, seven out of the ten were positive and three were negative for men; for the women, one was positive while five were negative. Thus, higher birth rates were associated more often with higher suicide rates in men, while higher birth rates were more often associated with lower suicide rates in women.

For divorce rates, twenty of the 23 associations were positive for men versus 15 for women. None of the gender differences were statistically significant. Among the significant coefficients, 12 were positive and one was negative for men; four were positive and none negative for women. Thus, the positive association between divorce and suicide rates was a little stronger for men than for women.

In summary, the association between marriage and suicide rates was negative in general for both men and women, a little more so for men than for women. Higher marriage rates were associated with lower suicide rates. The association between birth and suicide rates tended to be positive for men and negative for women. Finally, the association between divorce and suicide rates was positive for men and women, somewhat more so for men than for women.

These results provide some support for Gove's hypothesis about the benefits of marriage for men and women. In these 23 nations, using the present methodology, marriage had a slightly greater beneficial impact on suicide rates for men than for women.

REFERENCES

Chandler, C. R., & Tsai, Y. M. Suicide in Japan and in the West. *International Journal of Comparative Sociology,* 1993, 34, 244-259.

Doan, T. *Regression analysis of time series.* Evanston, IL: Var Econometrics, 1990.

Durkheim, E. *Le suicide.* Paris: Felix Alcan, 1897.

Gove, W. R. Sex differences in the epidemiology of mental disorder. In E. S. Gomberg & V. Franks (Eds.) *Gender and disordered behavior.* New York: Brunner/Mazel, 1979, 23-68.

Table 3.1

Results Of Time-Series Regressions For Men And Women, 1950-1985

	constant	marriage	birth	divorce	R^2	DW statistic
Men						
Australia	13.310*	-0.010	0.195	0.077	0.50	1.81
Austria	12.501	-0.729	0.596*	12.972*	0.80	2.06
Belgium	14.964	-0.889	0.448	8.728*	0.93	1.81
Canada	18.060*	-0.335	-0.1.98*	3.408*	0.98	1.65
Costa Rica	7.711*	-0.113	-0.057*	2.832	0.58	1.97
Denmark	24.479	0.464	-0.542	5.030	0.76	2.00
England/Wales	13.166*	-1.116*	0.389*	0.229	0.95	1.44
Finland	30.900*	-0.488	-0.020	6.407*	0.85	2.12
France	19.928*	-2.161*	0.838*	6.040*	0.94	2.14
Hungary	223.368*	-0.143	-0.528	0.903	0.96	2.30
Japan	-3.474	0.831	-0.325	19.355*	0.86	1.20
Luxembourg+	21.486	-0.817	-0.212	7.618*	0.66	1.85
Netherlands	1.589	0.165	0.141	4.371*	0.95	1.74
New Zealand	14.384*	-0.865	0.171	1.796*	0.53	2.03
N. Ireland	-4.886	-0.583	0.644*	7.517*	0.68	1.96
Norway	-1.664	-1.334*	0.912*	9.609*	0.95	1.91
Portugal	9.947*	-0.224	0.270*	1.620	0.33	1.91
Scotland	127.813*	0.273	0.074	-0.881	0.85	1.87
Sweden	15.598*	-1.167	1.404*	0.244	0.40	1.94
Switzerland	16.632	1.339	-0.418	8.967	0.84	1.98
USA	20.235*	-0.827*	0.005	1.457*	0.92	2.11
West Germany	34.098*	-0.830*	-0.030	-0.006	0.68	1.95
Yugoslavia	53.363*	-2.076*	-0.404*	-8.132*	0.91	1.32
Women						
Australia	6.525	-0.098	0.112	-0.423	0.79	1.72
Austria	13.108	0.937	-0.363	0.159	0.08	2.00
Belgium	18.837	-0.727	-0.426	3.408	0.92	2.05
Canada	2.588	0.549*	-0.137*	0.737*	0.97	1.78

Costa Rica	0.641	0.271	-0.039*	-0.007	0.60	1.79
Denmark	20.478*	-0.821	-0.192	2.280	0.89	1.94
England/Wales	4.972	-0.270	0.361*	-0.514	0.94	1.32
Finland	15.107*	-0.167	-0.262*	-0.210	0.72	2.37
France	3.518	-0.132	0.160	3.856*	0.95	1.95
Hungary	24.603*	0.011	-0.203	0.921	0.94	2.36
Japan	10.367	0.424	-0.189	1.411	0.88	1.25
Luxembourg+	20.070*	-1.476*	-0.223	0.356	0.57	2.00
Netherlands	9.237*	-0.117	-0.185	1.039	0.90	1.77
New Zealand	10.101*	0.182	-0.224*	-0.660	0.32	1.93
N. Ireland	-3.120	0.192	0.215	3.000*	0.41	1.93
Norway	-0.524	-0.125	0.128	3.743*	0.90	2.10
Portugal	6.102*	-0.115	-0.053	0.749	0.63	1.95
Scotland	0.232	0.329	0.129	1.152	0.61	2.35
Sweden	9.745*	-0.883*	0.438	0.235	0.83	2.22
Switzerland	8.565	0.651	-0.358	3.614	0.84	2.15
USA	10.616*	-0.007	-0.219*	-0.252	0.90	1.93
West Germany	14.352*	0.301	-0.155	-0.481	0.77	2.18
Yugoslavia	17.528*	-0.758*	-0.080	-1.231	0.78	1.70

* significant at the 5% level or better
+ interpolation was used for one year of missing suicide rates

Chapter Four

LETHAL VIOLENCE AND DOMESTIC INTEGRATION

Beguiled by Durkheim's (1897) theory of suicide, scholars have focused their research on an examination of the relationships between suicide rates and societal indicators of social integration and social regulation (such as divorce, marriage and birth rates), typically finding that societies with lower levels of social integration/regulation have higher rates of suicide. For example, in our study of time-series suicide rates in 29 nations in Chapter 2, we found that divorce rates were positively associated with suicide rates in the majority of nations, while marriage rates were negatively associated with suicide rates. Birth rates showed no consistent association with suicide rates.

Whitt, et al. (1972) suggested that it might be more meaningful to study the lethal violence rate in a society (that is, the sum of the suicide plus homicide rates) and the direction of aggression (that is, the difference between the suicide and homicide rates). How violent are societies, and in which direction do they direct their aggression? For example, in 1990, the United States had a suicide rate of 12.4 per 100,000 per year and a homicide rate of 9.9. The total lethal violence rate was, therefore, 22.3 and the direction score 2.5. In comparison, Italy had a suicide rate of 7.6, a homicide rate of 2.6, a lethal violence rate of 10.2 and a direction score of 5.0. Italy was, therefore, a less violent nation than America but relatively more aggressive inwardly.

The present study was undertaken to explore whether measures of domestic social integration (divorce, marriage and birth rates) predict lethal violence rates and the direction of violence.

The data set consisted of 19 nations with time-series data for suicide and homicide rates for 1950-1985. As in earlier analyses presented in this book, there was significant serial autocorrelation in the data sets, and so the Cochrane-Orcutt method was used to correct for this in the time-series regressions which were carried out using RATS (Doan, 1990).

The time-series regression results are shown in Table 4.1. It can be seen that divorce rates were positively associated with lethal violence rates for 13 of the 19 nations (one-tailed binomial p = .084). Ten of the eleven statistically significant regression coefficients were positive (p = .006).

Marriage rates were negatively associated with lethal violence rates for twelve of the 19 nations (p = .18) and all six statistically significant regression coefficients were negative (p = .016). Birth rates were positively associated with lethal violence rates for seven of the 19 nations (p = .18) and three of the seven statistically significant regression coefficients were positive (p = .227).

Thus, for lethal violence, the positive association of divorce rates and the negative association of marriage rates were moderately consistent. The association between lethal violence and birth rates was not as consistent.

With regard to direction of violence scores, 12 of the 19 regression coefficients for divorce were positive (p = .18) and ten of the 11 statistically significant coefficients positive (p = .006). Eleven of the 19 coefficients for marriage rates were negative (p = .084) and all six statistically significant coefficients were negative (p = .016). Twelve of the 19 coefficients for birth rates were positive (p = .18) and five of the six statistically significant coefficients were positive (p = .109). Thus, the direction of violence score was, on the whole, positively associated with divorce and birth rates and negatively with marriage rates.

The present study has shown that two measures of domestic social integration, namely divorce and marriage rates, are consistently associated with measures of lethal violence and the direction of violence scores of societies over time. Nations with high divorce rates and low marriage rates tend to experience higher rates of both lethal violence and inwardly-directed violence. Thus, Durkheim's theory of suicide may perhaps be legitimately extended in order to become a theory of lethal violence rather than being limited to suicide.

In the present study, the association between birth rates and lethal violence rates was less clear, but there was some tentative evidence that nations with higher birth rates also had higher rates of inwardly-directed violence.

The present study was limited by the absence of time-series homicide rates for nations where the homicide rate is relatively high, such as those in South America and Africa. It would be of great interest, were such data to become available, to examine the applicability of the ideas proposed in this paper to such nations.

REFERENCES

Doan, T. A. *Regression analysis of time series*. Evanston, IL: Var Econometrics, 1990.

Durkheim, E. *Le suicide*. Paris: Felix Alcan, 1897.

Whitt, H. P., Gordon, C. C., & Hofley, J. R. Religion, economic development and lethal aggression. *American Sociological Review*, 1972, 37, 193-201.

Table 4.1
Regression Analysis For Lethal Violence, 1950-1985

	divorce	marriage	birth	R^2
Lethal Violence				
Australia	-0.06	0.09	0.16	0.67
Belgium	4.97*	-1.27	0.30	0.95
Canada	2.27***	0.24	-0.24***	0.98
England/Wales	-0.05	-0.58	0.39**	0.93
Finland	3.38*	-0.37	-0.16	0.84
France	4.95***	-1.02*	0.45	0.94
Hungary	16.18***	-3.42**	1.39**	0.75
Iceland	-1.27	-0.16	-0.36	0.22
Japan	11.04*	0.62	-0.26	0.87
Netherlands	2.87***	0.05	-0.06	0.96
New Zealand	0.58	-0.41	-0.07	0.60
N. Ireland	-2.34	-3.46*	-1.44*	0.83
Norway	6.07***	-0.75*	0.37	0.96
Puerto Rico	1.98	0.58	-0.07	0.79
Sweden	0.57	-1.16*	1.00*	0.62
Switzerland	6.49*	1.10	-0.48	0.91
USA	1.32***	0.05	-0.36***	0.98
West Germany	-0.30	-0.78*	-0.05	0.80
Yugoslavia	-3.30**	-0.37	-0.18**	0.76
Direction of Violence				
Australia	-0.30	-0.07	0.20	0.71
Belgium	5.43**	-0.68	0.03	0.94
Canada	1.64***	0.02	-0.15	0.97
England/Wales	-0.09	-0.72	0.39*	0.95
Finland	3.85*	0.16	0.07	0.86
France	5.37***	-0.80*	0.46**	0.94
Hungary	17.56***	-1.49	0.26	0.80

Iceland	-4.71	-0.60	-0.60	0.17
Japan	9.58*	0.55	-0.24	0.86
Netherlands	2.55***	0.02	0.02	0.95
New Zealand	0.67*	-0.17	0.05	0.29
N. Ireland	9.60***	1.05	2.28***	0.86
Norway	5.40***	-0.82***	0.36	0.97
Puerto Rico	-1.12	-0.49	0.62*	0.87
Sweden	0.11	-1.00	0.94*	0.54
Switzerland	4.24	0.77	-0.50	0.87
USA	-0.58	-0.89**	-0.01	0.90
West Germany	-0.42	-0.72*	-0.03	0.79
Yugoslavia	-3.95***	-2.00***	-0.30***	0.95

*   p < .05
** p < .01
*** p < .001

Chapter Five

THE ASSOCIATION OF SUICIDE AND HOMICIDE OVER TIME IN NATIONS

Henry and Short (1954) hypothesized that the social conditions which increased the social suicide rate should decrease the social homicide rate, and *pari passu* social conditions which decreased the social suicide rate should increase the social homicide rate. This hypothesis was based on the assumption that suicide and homicide are both a result of frustration produced by social stressors. If the outward expression of the anger resulting from this frustration is legitimized, then assaultive and murderous behavior will result; if the outward expression of anger is prohibited, then the anger will be inhibited and turned inward on to the self, resulting in depression and suicidal behavior. Thus, the more anger is expressed outwardly, the less depression and suicidality there will be; the less anger is expressed outwardly, the more depression and suicidality there will be. As a result, homicide and suicide should be negatively associated in societies, both in cross-sectional (regional) studies and over time within a nation.[3]

---

[3] An assumption that seems to underlie Henry and Short's hypothesis that suicide and homicide rates should move in opposite directions is that the total aggression rate of a society, the suicide plus the homicide rate (which we called the lethal violence rate in Chapter 4), should stay constant.

To explore whether this hypothesis is useful, data on suicide and homicide rates were available for nineteen nations for the period 1950-1985. Table 5.1 shows the simple Pearson correlation coefficients for the association between suicide and homicide rates for these nations. Thirteen of the correlation coefficients were positive and six negative (two-tailed binomial p = .17). Fourteen of the correlation coefficients were statistically significant, eleven positive and three negative (binomial p = .058). Thus, the tendency was for positive associations to be more common than negative associations, in opposition to Henry and Short's hypothesis. Countries with higher rates of homicide tended to have higher rates of suicide -- not lower rates as predicted by Henry and Short.

The simple linear regressions of suicide rates on homicide rates gave identical results to those obtained in the simple correlational analysis, but there was serial autocorrelation in the data sets. The regression coefficients for the simple linear regression on suicide rates on homicides rates, correcting for the serial autocorrelation using the Cochrane-Orcutt technique (Doan, 1990), are also shown in Table 5.1. Thirteen of the regression coefficients were positive and six negative (binomial p = .17). Only seven were statistically significant, six positive and one negative (binomial p = .12). Again, a weak tendency toward a positive association was apparent in these results. Note that in two cases the correlational result was opposite to the regression result (Ireland and Yugoslavia).

Thus, the present data analyses indicate that Henry and Short's hypothesis about the inverse association between social suicide and homicide rates is not supported by time-series data from the majority of nations. This implies that (1) the total aggregate violence rate of a society caused by common stressors is not a constant, and (2) homicide and suicide may be caused by different sets of social stressors or, alternatively, two different sets of stressors with a limited overlap.

REFERENCES

Doan, T. A. *Regression analysis of time series.* Evanston, IL: Var Econometrics, 1990.

Henry, A. F., & Short, J. F. *Suicide and homicide*. New York: Free Press, 1954.

Table 5.1
The Association Between Suicide And Homicide Rates Over Time, 1950-
1985

	correlation coefficient	regression coefficient
Australia	-0.12	-0.96
Belgium	0.88*	1.08
Canada	0.95*	0.89
England/Wales	-0.74*	-0.37
Finland	0.34*	1.11*
France	0.25	0.04
Hungary	-0.18	-0.07
Iceland	-0.12	-0.71
Ireland	0.62*	-0.01
Japan	0.57*	9.10*
Netherlands	0.95*	2.84*
New Zealand	0.53*	1.00*
Northern Ireland	0.12	0.05
Puerto Rico	-0.49*	-0.22*
Sweden	0.33*	0.21
Switzerland	0.65*	0.03
USA	0.87*	0.34*
West Germany	0.80*	3.68*
Yugoslavia	-0.89*	0.18

* p < .05 or better

Chapter Six

CHANGING SUICIDE RATES IN THE TWENTIETH CENTURY

Lester (1992) reported that the suicide rates of nations (with data available) appeared to have increased from 1875 to 1975. The present note analyses data from twelve nations with reported suicide rates from 1901 to 1988 obtained from the World Health Organization, supplemented by official agencies in the nations (personal communications). The rates are presented in Appendix C.

Eight of the nations had positive Pearson correlation coefficients between year and suicide rates (see Table 6.1), while four had negative correlation coefficients. Multiple regressions using the Cochrane-Orcutt method to correct for serial autocorrelation (Doan, 1990) gave regression coefficients for suicide rates on year of identical signs to the Pearson correlation coefficients.

Thus, increasing suicide rates in modern times is found in some, but not all, nations with available data.

REFERENCES

Doan, T. A. *Regression analysis of time series*. Evanston, IL: Var Econometrics, 1990.

Lester, D. Have national suicide rates increased and converged over the last 100 years? *Perceptual & Motor Skills*, 1992, 75, 1262.

Table 6.1

Changes In Suicide Rates, 1901-1988

	regression coefficients (b) constant year		correlation with year Pearson r
Australia	11.10*	0.011	0.04
England/Wales	12.65*	-0.046	-0.31*
Finland	8.32*	0.214*	0.89*
Ireland	-0.31	0.075	0.45*
Italy	8.63*	-0.026	-0.41*
Netherlands	5.80*	0.041*	0.60*
New Zealand	11.99*	-0.021	-0.33*
Norway	0.74	0.149*	0.77*
Scotland	5.12*	0.060	0.57*
Spain	4.99*	0.008	0.26*
Sweden	13.91*	0.067*	0.72*
Switzerland	23.95*	-0.026	-0.21*

$p < .05$ or better

Chapter Seven

THE CONSISTENCY OF NATIONAL SUICIDE RATES

One noteworthy feature of the time-series suicide rates of nations is that, although they are somewhat consistent, they do vary a little from year to year. The present chapter explores differences between nations in this variation.

Data sets were developed, based primarily on World Health Organization (annual) data for suicide rates in 36 nations of the world for the period 1960 to 1990. The standard deviations of each nation's suicide rates over the 31 year period varied from 0.42 to 8.08 (mean = 2.35, SD = 1.60), and the coefficients of variation (100*sigma/mu) from 6.52 to 79.43 (mean = 20.68, SD = 15.44).

The Pearson correlation between the standard deviations of the suicide rates of the 36 nations and the mean suicide rates was 0.48 (one-tailed $p <$ 0.005), indicating that countries with a higher suicide rate tended to experience a greater variation in their suicide rates over the 31 year period. For example, four of the five countries with the highest suicide rates (Austria, Denmark, Finland, Hungary and Switzerland) had standard deviations greater than the average. In contrast, countries with very low suicide rates (such as Costa Rica, Greece, Ireland and Spain) had standard deviations less than the average.

The correlation between the standard deviations of the suicide rates of the 36 nations and the population in 1975 of the nations was -0.26 ($p < 0.10$), indicating that nations with a smaller population tended to experience a greater variation in their suicide rates over the 31 year period. For example, among the sample of countries, the two with the largest populations (Japan and the United States) had standard deviations less than the average. In contrast, the countries with the smallest populations (Liechtenstein, Iceland and Mauritius) had standard deviations greater than the average.

A regression equation with the nations' populations and suicide rates as explanatory variables was used to explain the dispersion of the suicide rates of the nations. The empirical result indicated that these two variables accounted for 30.2% of the variation over the 36 nations in the dispersions of their suicide rates. (The multiple correlation [R] was 0.55.)

To summarize, the more populous nations and those with lower suicide rates tended to have less variation in their suicide rates over the period 1960-1990, but these two predictors accounted for only 30 percent of the variation in the dispersion of the suicide rates.

REFERENCE

World Health Organization. *Statistics annual.* Geneva: World Health Organization, annual.

Table 7.1
Suicide rates, 1960-1990

	mean suicide rate	standard deviation	coefficient of variation	population in 1975
Australia	12.43	1.39	11.18	13.89
Austria	24.26	2.01	8.29	7.52
Belgium	19.97	3.42	19.03	9.79
Bulgaria	12.57	2.83	22.51	8.72
Canada	11.82	2.54	21.49	22.70
Costa Rica	3.84	1.12	29.17	1.97
Czechoslovakia	21.05	2.20	10.45	14.80
Denmark	23.93	3.99	16.67	5.06
England/Wales	9.00	1.40	15.56	49.16
Finland	23.79	2.92	12.27	4.71
France	17.71	2.76	15.58	52.70
Greece	3.45	0.42	12.17	9.05
Hong Kong	10.93	1.86	17.02	4.40
Hungary	37.55	7.01	18.67	10.53
Iceland	11.49	3.46	30.11	0.22
Ireland	4.70	2.37	50.43	3.18
Israel	6.47	0.82	12.67	3.46
Italy	6.33	1.01	15.96	55.83
Japan	17.45	2.05	11.74	111.57
Liechtenstein	12.58	8.08	64.23	0.02
Mauritius	5.59	4.44	79.43	0.88
Netherlands	8.88	1.86	20.95	13.65
New Zealand	10.35	1.80	17.39	3.09
North. Ireland	5.75	1.84	32.00	1.54
Norway	10.78	3.22	29.87	4.01
Poland	11.27	1.61	14.29	34.02
Portugal	8.79	0.77	8.76	9.43
Scotland	8.95	1.33	14.86	5.21

Singapore	10.12	1.63	16.11	2.26
Spain	5.13	1.21	23.59	35.60
Sweden	19.39	1.36	7.01	8.19
Switzerland	21.15	2.96	14.00	6.41
Taiwan	12.02	3.11	25.87	14.41
USA	11.81	0.77	6.52	215.97
West Germany	20.22	1.50	7.42	61.83
Yugoslavia	14.22	1.57	11.04	21.37

Chapter Eight

TRENDS IN NATIONAL SUICIDE RATES FROM 1960-1990: HAVE SUICIDE RATES PEAKED?

Lester (1990) reported that suicide rates appeared to have been increasing for the majority of nations for the period 1970-1984. For example, male suicide rates showed a positive linear regression trend (regressing the suicide rate on the year) in 21 of the 23 nations studied, and 18 of the 21 increasing trends were statistically significant. For women, there was an increasing trend in 14 nations (of which nine were statistically significant) and a decreasing trend in nine nations (of which five were statistically significant). However, later research suggested that the increase in suicide rates was slowing down in the 1980s (Lester, 1995).

The present analysis is of national suicide rates from 1960 to 1990 for 36 nations with available data. Regression analyses were run for suicide rate on year in two ways:

(1) a simple linear regression, providing an equation of the form

suicide rate = a + b.year + u

where a and b are parameters and u the disturbance term. Here, a positive b coefficient indicates an increasing trend over the period, while a negative b coefficient indicates a decreasing trend over the period.

(2) a multiple regression to identify quadratic trends, providing an equation of the form

$$\text{suicide rate} = c + d.\text{year} + e.\text{year2} + v$$

where c, d and e are parameters and the v the disturbance term. Here, a positive e coefficient indicates a U-shaped curve, while a negative e coefficient indicates an inverted U-shaped curve. An inverted U-shaped curve indicates that the suicide rate has peaked and is now declining (or increasing at a slower rate than before).

The coefficients relevant to these regressions are shown in Table 8.1. It can be seen from the estimates of the b coefficient of the linear trend that 28 of the 36 nations experienced a positive trend in the suicide rate (that is, an increasing suicide rate) during the period 1960-1990, 25 significantly so, while 8 nations experienced a decreasing trend, four significantly so.

However, looking at the coefficients for quadratic trends, it can be seen that 15 nations had negative e coefficients suggesting that suicide rates had peaked, 9 significantly so. Twenty-one nations had positive e coefficients, indicating that suicide rates in those nations were continuing to increase, 12 significantly so.

The nine nations with negative and statistically significant e coefficients were: Bulgaria, Canada, Czechoslovakia, Denmark, Hungary, Poland, Sweden, the United States and West Germany. The suicide rates peaked in the following year for these nations: Bulgaria 1987, Canada 1983, Czechoslovakia 1970, Denmark 1980, Hungary 1983/1984, Poland 1984, Sweden 1970, the United States 1977, and West Germany 1977.

The twelve nations with statistically significant positive e coefficients were: England/Wales, France, Greece, Ireland, Italy, Mauritius, New Zealand, Northern Ireland, Norway, Scotland, Spain, and Taiwan.

Comparing the suicide rates of these two groups of nations in 1960, the first group of nine nations with negative e coefficients had a mean suicide rate of 15.3 (standard deviation = 6.9), and the second of nations with positive e coefficients had a mean suicide rate of 7.7 (standard deviation = 4.5), a significant difference ($F1,19 = 9.51$, $p = 0.006$). Thus, this comparison indicates that nations whose suicide rate appears to have peaked in the 1980s had higher suicide rates in 1960 than those whose suicide rates have not yet peaked.

Other than this, since the countries in each group are widely scattered over the continents and the representatives from each continent are limited by the availability of data, we were not able to perceive any geographical pattern in the quadratic trend in the suicide rates.

Of course, more complicated analyses are possible. For example, a few of the time-series national suicide rates appeared to be best described by polynomials of degree three or four, but in most cases the regression coefficients for these analyses failed to reach statistical significance. However, for specifications of polynomials of degree three or four, a much longer period than 31 years may be necessary, requiring suicide rates well into the next century in order for reliable complex trends to be identified.

REFERENCES

Lester, D. Changes to suicide rates unique to Canada? *Canadian Journal of Public Health,* 1990, 81, 240-241.

Lester, D. Recent trends in national suicide rates. *Giornale Italiano di Suicidologia,* 1995, 5, 29-32.

Table 8.1
Regression coefficients for the regressions for 35 nations, 1960-1990

	linear trend b coefficient	quadratic trend e coefficient
Australia	-0.057*	+0.0062
Austria	+0.168*	-0.0012
Belgium	+0.323*	-0.0026
Bulgaria	+0.298*	-0.0055*
Canada	+0.244*	-0.0144*
Costa Rica	+0.101*	+0.0002
Czechoslovakia	-0.168*	-0.0152*
Denmark	+0.364*	-0.0128*
England/Wales	-0.111*	+0.0091*
Finland	+0.288*	+0.0022
France	+0.264*	+0.0094*
Hong Kong	+0.029	-0.0047
Hungary	+0.698*	-0.0343*
Ireland	+0.242*	+0.0066*
Greece	+0.010	+0.0040*
Iceland	+0.137*	+0.0054
Israel	-0.015	+0.0003
Italy	+0.094*	+0.0035*
Japan	+0.090*	+0.0080
Liechtenstein	+0.164	-0.0188
Mauritius	+0.328*	+0.2100*
Netherlands	+0.185*	-0.0035
New Zealand	+0.161*	+0.0094*
Northern Ireland	+0.119*	+0.0121*
Norway	+0.343*	+0.0059*
Poland	+0.147*	-0.0074*
Portugal	-0.011	+0.0008
Scotland	+0.118*	+0.0063*
Singapore	+0.111*	+0.0004

Spain	+0.081*	+0.0124*
Sweden	-0.035	-0.0121*
Switzerland	+0.267*	-0.0062
Taiwan	-0.273*	+0.0124*
USA	+0.070*	-0.0032*
West Germany	-0.015	-0.0180*
Yugoslavia	+0.160*	+0.0017

Chapter Nine

UNEMPLOYMENT AND SUICIDE/HOMICIDE

As we mentioned briefly in Chapter 2, Durkheim (1897) proposed that two characteristics of societies were central for the understanding of suicide: social integration and social regulation. The degree of *social integration* referred to the extent to which the members of a society shared beliefs and sentiments, interest in one another, and a shared sense of devotion to common goals. Later sociologists have stressed more the number, type, and durability of social relationships in a society as critical for the definition of social integration, such as marriage rates, church-attendance, community organizations, etc. Suicidal behavior is assumed to be frequent in societies where the level of social integration is very low, leading to *egoistic* suicide, and where the level of social integration is very high, leading to *altruistic* suicide.

The members of a society are *socially regulated* insofar as the society controls their emotions and motivations through social norms, customs and rules. Suicide will be common where social regulation is very low, leading to *anomic* suicide, and where social regulation is very high, leading to *fatalistic* suicide.

Durkheim considered the effects of the economy on suicide in his chapter on anomic suicide. He noted that financial crises led to an immediate rise in the suicide rate, but he also noted that suicide rates rose also during *fortunate crises* which enhanced a nation's prosperity. Durkheim concluded that financial crises do not lead to a higher suicide rate because of the increased poverty, but rather because they disturb the *collective order*.

Durkheim suggested that people differ from other animals in that their desires often outstrip the means at their disposal for satisfying them. He felt that people's desires easily become unlimited and, therefore, insatiable. The only check on these desires is from external sources which must provide the moral forces to restrain their desires, and only society can play this moderating role. Society must set a limit on desires and must also estimate the appropriate rewards for its members.

Economic disasters cast some people into lower statuses in which they must restrain their desires still further and accept still fewer rewards. But the speed of such disasters gives the society no time to prepare its members for such abrupt changes. Since the people cannot adjust quickly to the new conditions, their suffering is increased. Similarly, during periods of prosperity, the conditions of life change without adequate time for the society to prepare the members of the society for this change. The increasing prosperity removes the limits on people's desires without new limits being imposed. There is no restraint upon aspirations. In both of these types of crisis (disasters and prosperity), the result is a reduction in the strength of social regulation and an accompanying increase in anomie which is conducive to suicidal behavior.

Thus, Durkheim's theory results in a U-shaped function relating the economy and suicide, specifically a U-shaped relationship between the rate of economic change and the suicide rate. Suicide is more common during times of both extreme economic contraction and economic expansion and less common in times of normal and moderate economic activity.

GINSBERG

Ginsberg (1966) reinterpreted Durkheim's notion of anomie in terms of the psychological discrepancy between the levels of aspiration and rewards.

Ginsberg noted that anomie arose from the unhappiness or dissatisfaction of individuals. He postulated further that the dissatisfaction of the individual was a direct function of the discrepancy between the actual reward that the individual was receiving and his level of aspiration. In the *normal process*, internalized legitimate norms which are dependent upon the individual's social position regulate changes in the individual's level of aspiration. The level of aspiration remains proportional to the rewards and the individual is relatively satisfied. In the *anomic process*, the level of aspiration, freed from external constraints, runs away from the rewards, resulting in unhappiness for the individual.

Ginsberg formalized Durkheim's implicit propositions as follows: (a) as rewards increase, aspirations tend to increase, and as rewards decrease, aspirations tend to decrease, and (b) the rate of change of aspirations is a function of the extent to which rewards increase or decrease.

Ginsberg suggested that, if an individual sees no relationship between what he does and the rewards he obtains, then there is no tendency for aspirations to change. For the level of aspiration to change, the individual must possess and feel a *sense of efficacy*. As the individual's sense of efficacy increases, his aspirations tend to drop. The sense of efficacy is an intervening variable between changes in his rewards and his level of aspirations.

When rewards increase faster than aspirations, we have a normal process, but when aspirations increase faster than rewards, we have an anomic process. In the anomic process aspirations mount at an increasingly faster rate, running away from rewards, and this is what happens to some individuals during financial booms. Similarly, when rewards decrease and aspirations decrease at a lesser rate, leveling off at some constant value and converging with rewards, we have a normal process. When aspirations decrease at an increasing rate and never reach an equilibrium with rewards, we have an anomic process, and this is what happens to some individuals during financial crashes.

Ginsberg attempted to deduce the discrepancy between aspirations and rewards at different points of the business cycle and to predict the association between business prosperity and the suicide rate. In formal terms, Ginsberg assumed that (a) the suicide rate in a given society varied directly with the average amount of dissatisfaction in that society, (b) fluctuations in the economy determine the average rewards available, (c) the average dissatisfaction depends upon the average aspirations as well as the average rewards, and (d) economic aspirations are governed by the following five postulates:

(1) When rewards are increasing, the individual will expect them to continue to increase and raise his aspirations accordingly.

(2) As long as the rate of change of rewards is increasing and as long as rewards are cumulative, the individual will expect them to continue to cumulate and raise his aspirations to meet the even higher expected rewards.

(3) When rewards are decreasing, the individual will expect them to continue to decrease and lower his aspirations accordingly.

(4) As long as the rate of fall of rewards is increasing and as long as the drops are cumulative, the individual will expect them to continue to cumulate and lower his aspirations to meet the even lower expected rewards.

(5) When the rate of change in rewards is decreasing, the rate of change of aspiration will decrease even faster in anticipation of the end of the trend.

According to these assumptions, we may infer that, when the economy is expanding at an increasing rate during the course of prosperity, aspirations are raised to a level which causes an ever-increasing discrepancy between aspirations and individual rewards. On the other hand, when the economic is contracting at a decreasing rate during the course of a recession, aspirations are lowered to a level which closes the ever narrowing gap between aspirations and rewards.

Thus, Ginsberg's theory predicts a positive association between economic prosperity and the suicide rate based on points (1) and (2) above.

HENRY AND SHORT

Henry and Short (1954) made two major predictions concerning the relationship between the business cycle and suicide and homicide rates: (a) Suicide rates will rise during times of business depression and fall during times of business prosperity, while crimes of violence against people will rise during business prosperity and fall during business depressions, and (b) the correlation between suicide rates and the business cycle will be higher for high status groups than for low status groups, while the correlation between homicide rates and the business cycle will be higher for low status groups than for high status groups.

Henry and Short interpreted their predictions in terms of the frustration-aggression hypothesis (Dollard, et al., 1939). Their assumptions were (a) aggression is often a consequence of frustration, (b) business cycles produce variations in the hierarchical rankings of persons by status, and (c) frustrations are generated by a failure to maintain a constant or rising position in the status hierarchy relative to the status position of other groups.

Their interpretation required two additional assumptions: (a) high status persons lose status relative to low status persons during business contraction while low status persons lose status relative to high status persons during business expansions, and (b) suicide, an inwardly-directed aggression, occurs mainly in high status persons while homicide, an outwardly-directed aggression, occurs mainly in low status persons.

Consider those who lose income during business contraction. The high status person has more income to lose than the low status person. The high status person loses status relative to the low status person. The low status person may actually experience a gain in status relative to the high status person. Thus in times of business contraction, high status people lose status relative to low status people, and this generates frustration. The aggression consequent to this frustration in high status people is predominantly self-directed aggression, and so suicide rates rise in times of business contraction in high status people. This analysis explains why suicide rates and the business cycle are negatively correlated in whites, a high status group.

During times of business expansion, high status persons gain more income than low status persons and experience a relative gain in status over low status persons (and *pari passu* low status persons experience a relative loss of status compared to high status persons). This leads to low levels of frustration in high status persons and an increase in frustration in low status persons. Thus, in times of business expansion, the suicide rate decreases and the homicide rate increases.

Thus, Henry and Short's theory predicts that suicide and the business cycle are related by a monotonic negative function -- suicide rates increase as the economy worsens.

EMPIRICAL TESTS OF THESE THEORIES[4]

The majority of empirical examinations of the relationship between the economy and the suicide rate have looked for simple linear relationships, using unemployment as an indicator of economic conditions (for an expanding economy tends to generate a lower unemployment rate, while a contracting economy tends to generate a high unemployment rate). For example, Yang and Lester (1995) examined the linear regression of the suicide rate on the unemployment rate in twelve nations for the period 1950-1985 and found nine positive associations and three negative associations, although the four significant associations were all positive. The present analyses, however, were conducted to explore whether the relationship was linear as Ginsberg and Henry and Short predicted or curvilinear as Durkheim predicted.

Data were available for fourteen nations for the period 1950-1985. The unemployment rate was utilized here as a measure of the economy, although of course other measures are possible (such as the inflation rate). Two sets of results are presented: (1) the results of linear regressions of the suicide rate on the unemployment rate and (2) the results of regressions of the suicide rate on the unemployment rate and the square of the unemployment rate in order to explore quadratic trends. Here, the U-shaped relationship between the economy and the suicide rate should be replaced by an inverted U-shaped relationship between the unemployment rate and the suicide rate.

LINEAR TRENDS

An examination of the linear regressions (see Table 9.1) indicated some support for an increasing monotonic function. The regression coefficient was positive for ten of the fourteen nations in both the simple linear regressions and the regressions using the Cochrane-Orcutt technique to correct for the serial autocorrelation in the data.

---

[4] For a mathematical formulation of these three theories see Lester and Yang (1997)

QUADRATIC TRENDS

An examination of the empirical results of the tests for quadratic trends (see Table 9.2) indicated that only a few nations experienced a significant quadratic trend, and only one after correction for serial autocorrelation.

CONCLUSION

The data for these fourteen nations for the period 1950-1985 support a trend for suicide rates to rise as the unemployment rate increases, in line with Henry and Short's theory. Of course, the results might differ if transformations of the data were attempted (such as a logarithmic transformation) and if other variables were included in the regressions. However, without some evidence of a relationship easily noted, these refinements would be unconvincing.

GENDER DIFFERENCES

From an economic point of view, the marginal impact of loss of income is expected to be greater for men than for women if the utility function of income is assumed to be the same for both genders. This is based on the observation that the wage compensation for women tends to be about 25% to 40% less than that for men with the same qualifications. When layoffs occur, the loss of income is greater for men than for women. As a result, we may conclude that unemployment might have a greater social impact (including economic impact) on men than on women.

To answer this question, the association between unemployment rates and gender-specific suicide rates were examined for eleven nations for the period 1950-1985. Looking at Pearson correlation coefficients, all eleven nations had higher correlations between unemployment rates and suicide rates for men than for women (see Table 9.3).

In multiple regressions, using the Cochrane-Orcutt method to correct for the serial autocorrelation in the data sets, the regression coefficient for male suicide rates was greater than that for female suicide rate for ten of the eleven nations. (The exception was Norway.) Three nations had significant positive regression coefficients for male suicide rates (Japan, the Netherlands, and the United States) while only two had significant positive regression coefficients for female suicide rates (the Netherlands and Norway). Thus, by and large, it does appear that unemployment had a greater impact on male suicide rates than on female suicide rates during the period studied.

CONTROLS FOR DIVORCE

Since the divorce rate is a strong correlate of suicide rates, we used both unemployment and divorce rates as explanatory variables for the suicide rate in order to see whether unemployment rates were still significantly associated with suicide rates after divorce rates (a strong correlate of suicide rates) was controlled for. The results of multiple regressions for thirteen countries for the period 1950-1985 are shown in Table 9.4.

Looking at the multiple regressions, among the thirteen countries, Taiwan is the only country for which the unemployment rate was the sole significant predictor of the suicide rate. For four countries (Austria, Belgium, Canada and the Netherlands), only the divorce rate was a significant predictor of the suicide rate. For Denmark, Norway and the United States, however, both the unemployment rate and the divorce rate were significant predictors of the suicide rate. For these nations, the impact of divorce on the suicide rate seems to be greater than the impact of unemployment.

When the results shown in Table 9.4 and Table 9.1 are compared, it can be seen that the significant impact of unemployment on suicide for Japan and the Netherlands indicated in Table 9.1 is eliminated when divorce is entered into the prediction equation as in Table 9.4. Thus, for these nations, domestic social integration seems to be more important as an explanatory variable than economic conditions. However, for Denmark, Norway and Taiwan, the addition of the divorce rate into the regression equation led to unemployment now becoming a significant predictor. Thus, the relative roles of domestic social integration and economic conditions vary greatly from nation to nation.

HOMICIDE AND UNEMPLOYMENT

The simple Pearson correlations between homicide rates and unemployment rates for ten countries with available data are presented in Table 9.5. Eight of the ten correlations were positive (Australia, Belgium, Canada, England/Wales, Ireland, the Netherlands, Norway, Sweden, the United States and West Germany), and two were negative (Japan and West Germany). Five of the positive correlations were statistically significant (Belgium, Canada, Ireland, Norway and the United States); while one negative correlation was also statistically significant (Japan).

When time-series simple linear regressions were run for homicide with the unemployment rate as the sole predictor (see Table 9.5), six of the ten regression coefficients were positive, though only one was statistically significant (surprisingly that for Japan).

Time-series regressions were also run including divorce rates as well, since earlier preliminary research had indicated that divorce rates were a consistent contributor to multiple regressions on homicide rates. In this set of regression analyses, Ireland was omitted since there was no divorce possible in Ireland during this time period. As expected, all nine of the regression coefficients for divorce were positive, and six were statistically significant (see Table 9.5). However, for unemployment rates, six of the nine regression coefficients were positive (Australia, Belgium, Canada, Japan, Sweden, the United States and West Germany) and three negative (England/Wales, the Netherlands and Norway), but only the regression coefficients for England/Wales and the Netherlands were statistically significant, both negative.

The results of this study, therefore, provide little support for an association of unemployment rates with homicide rates in the ten nations studied. Although the simple correlation coefficients were positive on the whole, as predicted, more complex time-series multiple regression analysis failed to confirm this positive association. Thus, it must be concluded that unemployment and homicide rates are not associated in this sample of nations.

However, these results bring to mind what we have observed as an intriguing phenomenon in the comparison of time-series versus cross-sectional data analyses. Sometimes, both types of analysis result in different conclusions (e.g, B. Lester, 1996; Klein, 1960). Klein used income-expenditure data to show that cross-sectional analyses tend to reveal long-term relationships, while time-series tend to reveal short-term relationships. When B. Lester (1996) analyzed part-time employment of married women in the 48 contiguous states in 1980, she reached a similar conclusion. Therefore, we are not surprised than unemployment and homicide are not strongly positively associated in time-series national data, contrary to our expectations, since these analyses may be tapping only short-term relationships.

DISCUSSION

Three theories of the impact of the economy on suicide were reviewed. Durkheim's theory implied a U-shaped relationship between the rate of economic change and the suicide rate. Suicide is predicted to be more common during times of both economic expansion and contraction and less in times of normal economic activity. Ginsberg's reinterpretation of Durkheim's notion of anomie resulted in the prediction of a positive association between economic prosperity and the suicide rate. Henry and Short's theory predicted that suicide rates would rise during times of business recession and fall during times of business prosperity. Durkheim predicted a curvilinear relationship between the economy and suicide, whereas Ginsberg and Henry/Short predicted linear relationships, with positive and negative signs respectively.

Since the unemployment rate is a barometer of the economic health of a nation, we tend to link it to any social deviance. Yet we must remember that social deviance is the result of a combination of social and economic factors. As a result, it is not surprising that all three types of linkage may be found in some of any sample of nations. In the present set of analyses, the regression analyses indicated more support for a positive association between unemployment and suicide than for a negative association (from an inspection of the statistically significant regression coefficients in Tables 9.1 and 9.4), and thus Ginsberg's theory received the more support than Henry and Short's theory.

REFERENCES

Dollard, J., Doob, L.,Miller, N., Mowrer, O. H., & Sears, R. *Frustration and aggression*. New Haven: Yale University Press, 1939.

Durkheim, E. *Le suicide*. Paris: Felix Alcan, 1897.

Ginsberg, R. B. Anomie and aspirations. *Dissertation Abstracts*, 1966, 27A, 3945-3946.

Henry, A. F., & Short, J. F. *Suicide and homicide*. New York: Free Press, 1954.

Klein, L. R. *An introduction to econometrics*. Englewood Cliffs, NJ: Prentice-Hall, 1960.

Lester, B. Y. A cross-sectional analysis of part-time employment of married women in the U.S.A. *American Journal of Economics & Sociology*, 1996, 55, 61-72.

Lester, D., & Yang, B. *The economy and suicide: Economic perspectives on suicide*. Commack, NY: Nova Science, 1997.

Yang, B., & Lester, D. Suicide, homicide and unemployment. *Applied Economics Letters*, 1995, 2, 278-279.

Table 9.1

Linear Regressions For Unemployment On The Suicide Rate, 1950-1985

Simple Linear Regression

	constant	unemployment	R^2	DW statistic	Pearson Correlation
Australia	12.398*	-0.157	0.06	0.43	
Austria	23.729*	0.023	0.01	0.33	0.03
Belguim	12.120*	0.680*	0.50	0.22	0.71*
Canada	4.866*	0.893*	0.54	0.24	0.73*
Denmark	19.612*	0.563*	0.24	0.40	0.49*
England/Wales	10.712*	-0.281*	0.28	0.13	-0.53
Ireland	0.929	0.517*	0.69	0.66	0.83*
Japan	16.461*	1.414	0.06	0.16	0.24
Netherlands	6.740*	0.359	0.74	0.31	0.86*
Norway	8.715*	0.213	0.01	0.07	0.06
Sweden	20.211	-0.580	0.04	0.52	-0.21
Taiwan	8.575*	2.545*	0.53	0.55	0.73*
USA	9.225*	0.368*	0.48	0.46	0.69*
West Germany	20.077*	-0.002	0.01	0.25	-0.04

Cochrane-Orcutt Method

	constant	unemployment	R^2	DW statistic
Australia	12.205*	-0.004	0.67	1.77
Austria	24.217*	0.173	0.69	2.52
Belgium	113.704*	0.029	0.93	2.22
Canada	15.433*	0.110	0.97	1.46
Denmark	24.632*	-0.032	0.77	1.98
England/Wales	8.492*	-0.029	0.93	1.22
Ireland	16.289	0.075	0.89	2.53
Japan	13.860*	2.322*	0.86	1.61

Netherlands	8.244*	0.174*	0.94	1.78
Norway	-3.221	0.174	0.94	2.46
Sweden	20.509*	-0.574	0.54	2.10
Taiwan	8.782*	2.545*	0.79	2.07
USA	10.737*	0.133*	0.86	2.02
West Germany	19.969*	0.124	0.77	2.04

* p < .05 or better

Table 9.2

Curvilinear regressions For Unemployment On The Suicide Rate, 1950-1985

Simple Linear Regression

	constant	unemployment	square	R^2	DW statistic
Australia	12.622*	-0.299	0.015	0.07	0.42
Austria	22.127*	0.806	0.091	0.05	0.38
Belgium	15.795*	-0.545	0.079*	0.58	0.28
Canada	3.348	1.390	-0.035	0.55	0.27
Denmark	16.848	1.600	-0.077	0.26	0.42
England/Wales	13.018*	-1.571	0.113*	0.55	0.44
Ireland	-1.573	0.650	-0.006	0.69	0.67
Japan	8.057	12.553	3.276	0.14	0.21
Netherlands	5.767*	0.733*	-0.022*	0.80	0.59
Norway	7.516*	1.434	-0.277	0.01	0.07
Sweden	20.635*	-1.001	0.098	0.04	0.52
Taiwan	5.211*	7.150*	-1.291	0.56	0.64
USA	8.153*	0.752	-0.032	0.49	0.46
West Germany	19.468*	0.434	-0.045	0.07	0.27

Cochrane-Orcutt Method

	constant	unemployment	square	R^2	DW statistic
Australia	12.301*	-0.061	0.005	0.67	1.77
Austria	23.171	0.616	-0.038	0.69	2.57
Belgium	100.108*	0.065	-0.002	0.93	2.33
Canada	16.517*	-0.392	0.037	0.97	1.40
Denmark	23.736*	0.250	-0.019	0.77	1.97
England/Wales	8.927*	-0.084	0.005	0.93	1.22
Ireland	7.231	-0.121	0.010	0.89	2.46
Japan	14.455*	1.072	0.412	0.86	1.59

Netherlands	11.505*	-0.203	0.017*	0.95	1.63
Norway	-5.963	0.920	-0.151	0.94	2.44
Sweden	21.297*	-1.373	0.186	0.54	2.10
Taiwan	9.182*	1.950	0.183	0.79	2.09
USA	9.983*	0.407	-0.022	0.87	2.25
West Germany	19.750*	0.279	-0.017	0.77	2.05

* $p < .05$ or better

Table 9.3

Unemployment And Suicide By Gender, 1950-1985[#]

	suicide rates		
	total	male	female
Pearson Correlations			
Australia	-0.25	0.06	-0.45*
Belgium	0.71*	0.77*	0.59*
Canada	0.73*	0.79*	0.53*
Denmark	0.49*	0.60*	0.27
England/Wales	-0.53*	-0.37*	-0.67*
Ireland	0.83*	0.83*	0.77*
Japan	0.24	0.45*	-0.16
Netherlands	0.86*	0.90*	0.78*
Norway	0.06	0.09	-0.01
Taiwan	0.73*	-	-
USA	0.69*	0.80*	0.26
West Germany	-0.01	0.22	-0.38*
Regression (with Cochrane-Orcutt technique)			
Australia	-0.004	0.080	-0.074
Belgium	0.029	0.091	0.067
Canada	0.110	0.269	-0.044
Denmark	-0.032	0.074	-0.078
England/Wales	-0.029	0.071	-0.147
Ireland	0.075	0.102	0.073
Japan	2.322*	4.172*	0.730
Netherlands	0.174*	0.245*	0.158*
Norway	0.174	-0.278	0.617*
Taiwan	2.545*	-	-
USA	0.133*	0.217*	0.031
West Germany	0.124	0.316	-0.051

* two-tailed p < .05

[#] Suicide rates by gender for Taiwan were not available

Table 9.4
Time-Series Regressions Of The Suicide Rate On Divorce And
Unemployment Rates, 1950-1985

regression coefficients
(with Cochrane-Orcutt technique)

	unemployment	divorce	constant	R^2
Australia	0.013	-0.315	12.619*	0.68
Austria	0.041	5.625*	15.727*	0.80
Belgium	0.101	5.971*	10.717*	0.95
Canada	0.108	1.712*	7.786	0.97
Denmark	0.382*	4.559*	11.640*	0.84
England/Wales	-0.001	-0.541	10.495*	0.93
Japan	1.834	5.543	7.270	0.86
Netherlands	0.023	2.610*	5.219*	0.96
Norway	0.340*	5.255*	3.046*	0.96
Sweden	-0.575	0.050	20.417	0.54
Taiwan	2.563*	-2.053	9.901*	0.79
USA	0.118*	0.578*	8.604*	0.89
West Germany	0.155	-0.459	20.458*	0.77

* significant at the 5% level or better

Table 9.5

Time-Series Regression Analyses For Homicide On Unemployment, 1950-
1985

Simple Regression And Correlation

Regression coefficients

	constant	unemployment	R^2	Pearson Correlation
Australia	1.637*	0.010	0.63	0.56
Belgium	25.934	-0.013	0.80	0.68*
Canada	1.822*	0.041	0.92	0.67*
England/Wales	0.778*	0.016	0.64	0.29
Ireland	0.038	0.146	0.25	0.40*
Japan	-3.329*	0.199*	0.96	-0.55*
Netherlands	0.527*	0.016	0.91	0.78
Norway	0.733*	-0.015	0.69	0.34*
Sweden	1.033*	-0.024	0.63	0.30
USA	10.375*	0.019	0.96	0.54*
West Germany	1.112*	0.008	0.64	-0.07

Multiple Regression (with Cochrane-Orcutt technique)

Regression coefficients

	constant	unemployment	divorce	R^2
Australia	1.328*	0.004	0.183*	0.77
Belgium	0.315*	0.003	0.712*	0.83
Canada	1.113*	0.029	0.386*	0.93
England/Wales	0.477*	-0.057**	0.264*	0.71
Japan	-18.122*	0.163	0.482	0.96
Netherlands	0.108*	-0.016*	0.459*	0.93
Norway	0.308	-0.014	0.382*	0.73
Sweden	0.266*	0.042	0.319	0.77
USA	1.472	0.032	1.517*	0.97
West Germany	1.060*	0.003	0.052	0.64

* two-tailed $p < .05$ or better

Chapter Ten

SUICIDE RATES FROM 1751 TO 1988

So far in this book, we have examined changes in the suicide rates of nations from 1950 to 1985 (as in Chapter 2). Some nations have time-series suicide rates going back much further in time. For instance, Finland's suicide rates are available back to 1751, Sweden's 1776, and Switzerland's 1876. Therefore, in this chapter, we will explore the extent to which measures of social integration are associated with suicide rates for these nations over these longer periods of time.

FINLAND

Finland's suicide rate over the last 230 years has been examined before (Lester, 1992; Stack, 1993). Stack (1993) found that urbanization was positively associated with the Finnish suicide rate from 1800 to 1984, while Lester (1992) found that the Finnish suicide rate from 1933 to 1985 could be predicted using variables related to social integration as predicted by Durkheim's (1897) theory of suicide, namely divorce, marriage and birth rates, the same variables which were used in Chapter 2 of the present book. The Finnish suicide rate during this period was positively associated with the divorce rate and negatively associated with the marriage and birth rates. Thus, the greater the degree of social integration, the lower the Finnish suicide rate in this period, results which confirm Durkheim's theory.

In seeking to explore correlates of the Finnish suicide rate over longer periods of time, we are limited by the availability of data -- only marriage and birth rates were available for Finland for the period of 1751 to 1988 (Mitchell, 1992). Suicide rates by gender for Finland from 1751 to the present day were obtained from the Central Statistical Office of Finland with the aid of Steven Stack (Wayne State University). A plot of these historical time-series data shows that the suicide rate in Finland has increased since 1751, while the birth rate has declined over the same period of time. The long-term trend in the Finnish marriage rate appears to be a decline, but much less steep than for the birth rate.

The data were analyzed with simple Pearson correlations and with time-series multiple regressions using the Cochrane-Orcutt technique to correct for the serial autocorrelation in the data (Doan, 1990). The data were analyzed for successive 50 year periods, 1751 to 1800, 1801 to 1850 etcetera. The results are shown in Table 10.1.

It can be seen that more of the Pearson correlation coefficients were statistically significant for the later periods than for the earlier periods. For example, no correlation coefficient was statistically significant for the period 1751 to 1800, while birth and marriage rates were significantly associated with suicide rates for the period 1951 to 1988.

The marriage rate was negatively associated with the suicide rate in recent times, while the birth rate was negatively associated with the suicide rate since 1851, although there were gender differences in these associations.

Thus, Durkheim's theory was confirmed most clearly for the most modern period, 1951 to 1988. There was less support for the periods 1801 to 1850, 1851 to 1900 and 1901 to 1950 and no support for the earliest period, 1751 to 1800. We can conclude, therefore, that Durkheim's theory of suicide is most appropriately applied to the Finnish suicide rate only since the Second World War. Alternative theories may be required for earlier periods. Furthermore, the differences in the results for male and female suicide rates are of interest.

Looking at the time-series regressions in Table 10.1, the social indicators appear to be more successful in accounting for the male suicide rates than for the female suicide rates (as indicated by the multiple R^2 values). This may be because the male rates are higher (and, therefore, more reliable rates), or it may be that different social factors from those used in the present study would predict the female suicide rate more precisely. Further research is required to test these possibilities.

In order to explore whether the results look different for other divisions of the 238-year time period, analyses were run for the total suicide rate for three periods:(1) 1751-1808, the period of Swedish-Russian conflict, (2) 1810-1913 the period of Russian influence prior to the First World War, and (3) 1919-1988, the period of independence after the First World War. These results are shown in Table 10.1.

It can be seen that the results differ somewhat. In the simple correlational analysis, the negative association between the birth rate and the suicide rate is generally replicated. However, the negative association between the marriage rate and the suicide rate was somewhat more consistent. In the regression analyses, the longer time periods improved the success of the social indicators in predicting the suicide rates, except for the period of Swedish-Russian conflict.

Of course, it may be that the accuracy of the official Finnish suicide rate is not consistent over the period studied, and we might suspect that it is more accurate in recent years than in the past. Any inaccuracies would militate against finding significant associations in the present study. However, there are no data available at present to argue for or against the accuracy of the official Finnish suicide rate in previous centuries, and so we must await further research before concluding that this is a critical issue.

SWEDEN

Suicide rates in Sweden, overall and for men and women separately, from 1776 to 1970 were obtained from Pers-Anders Linden of Stockholm University. These rates were calculated based on the population over the age of fifteen, unlike other suicide rates utilized so far in this book which have been based on the total population. As before, birth and marriage rates were obtained from Mitchell (1992) and the regressions run using the statistical package from Doan (1990) with the Cochrane-Orcutt technique to correct for serial autocorrelation. The results are shown in Table 10.2.

The results indicate strong associations between birth and marriage rates, in the direction predicted by Durkheim's theory of suicide, for all periods except 1776-1825. Again, therefore, Durkheim's theory does not appear to apply as well to earlier centuries.

SWITZERLAND

Suicide rates for Switzerland were available from Waldstein (1934) for 1876-1900 and from the World Health Organization for 1901-1988. Marriage and birth rates for this period were obtained from Mitchell (1992) who presented data up until 1988.

The total period was divided into three roughly equal periods, 1876-1912, 1913-1950, and 1951-1988, and the analyses carried out for each period. Pearson correlations and multiple regressions were run, correcting for the serial autocorrelation in the data sets using the Cochrane-Orcutt technique (Doan, 1990). The results are shown in Table 10.3.

Looking at the Pearson correlations, it can be seen that the negative association between birth rates and suicide was negative in all three time periods, but statistically significant only for 1951-1988. In the regressions, the association was positive for the period 1913-1950.

The association between marriage rates and suicide rates was negative for 1876-1912 and 1951-1988 but positive for 1913-1950. In the regressions, the association was positive only for 1951-1988.

The presence of children was thought by Durkheim to increase the level of domestic social integration and to be associated with lower suicide rates. This was evidently so for Switzerland in recent years (1951-1988), but not found in earlier times, at the end of the last century or at the beginning of the present century.

Marriage was thought also by Durkheim to increase the level of domestic social integration and to be associated with lower suicide rates. This seemed to be so for 1876-1912, but not found later in the present century.

It is clear, therefore, the pattern of results and, therefore, support for Durkheim's theory depends critically upon the time period chosen for study. The results for each time period studied in the present paper also differ considerably from the results for the total period, 1876-1988.

COMMENT

The social indicators used in the present studies (as well as other possible social indicators) may have different meanings in different eras. For example, as divorce becomes more common, many marriages are remarriages, whereas in earlier times, when divorce was rare, almost all marriages were first-time marriages. Similarly, birth rates may have a different social meaning in times when infant and child mortality was common than in times when infant and child mortality is greatly reduced. Further research is needed to explore the possible social meanings of the social indicators used in the present studies and how their meanings affect their associations with the suicide rate.

REFERENCES

Doan, T. A., *Regression analysis of time series.* Evanston, IL: Var Econometrics, 1990.

Durkheim, E. *Le suicide.* Paris: Felix Alcan, 1897.

Lester, D. The relationship between family integration and suicide and homicide in Finland and the USA. *Psychiatria Fennica,* 1992, 23, 23-27.

Mitchell, B. R. *International historical statistics: Europe 1750-1988.* New York: Stockton Press, 1992.

Stack, S. The effect of modernization on suicide in Finland. *Sociological Perspectives,* 1993, 36, 137-148.

Waldstein, E. *Der Selbstmord in der Schweiz.* Basle: Philographischer Verlag, 1934.

Table 10.1
Associations Of Marriage And Birth Rates With Suicide Rates In Finland

Pearson Correlations

	Birth	marriage
total suicide rate		
1751-1800	-0.02	-0.02
1801-1850	-0.22	0.04
1851-1900	-0.48#	-0.41#
1901-1950	-0.80#	0.44#
1951-1988	-0.85#	-0.70#
1751-1988	-0.94#	-0.26#
1751-1808	-0.16	-0.15
1810-1913	-0.59#	-0.51#
1919-1988	-0.79#	-0.37#
1919-1938	-0.67#	0.25
1946-1988	-0.89#	-0.74#
male suicide rate		
1751-1800	0.05	0.04
1801-1850	-0.18	0.05
1851-1900	-0.40#	-0.41#
1901-1950	-0.79#	0.44#
1951-1988	-0.83#	-0.74#
female suicide rate		
1751-1800	-0.11	-0.13
1801-1850	-0.29	-0.01
1851-1900	-0.44#	-0.16
1901-1950	-0.78#	0.43#
1951-1988	-0.82#	-0.58#

two-tailed p < .01

Multiple Regression Analysis

	constant	birth	marriage	R^2
total suicide rate				
1751-1988	126.457	0.028	-0.013	0.98
1751-1800	1.811	-0.011	-0.007	0.05
1801-1850	2.004	-0.024	0.100	0.38
1851-1900	8.593*	-0.129*	-0.013	0.41
1901-1950	13.726*	0.445*	-0.361	0.88
1951-1988	38.422*	-0.524*	-0.509*	0.85
1751-1808	2.626*	-0.023	-0.020	0.10
1810-1913	39.139	-0.104*	0.144*	0.82
1919-1988	21.694*	0.096	-0.010	0.85
1919-1938	26.757*	0.018	-0.428	0.82
1946-1988	38.217*	-0.554*	-0.466*	0.89
male suicide rate				
1751-1800	1.912	0.007	-0.011	0.01
1801-1850	1.968	-0.014	0.203	0.37
1851-1900	13.460*	-0.145	-0.125	0.34
1901-1950	23.202*	1.048*	-0.846*	0.90
1951-1988	63.670*	-0.803*	-0.980*	0.84
female suicide rate				
1751-1800	1.346	-0.014	-0.013	0.04
1801-1850	1.797*	-0.045	0.031	0.10
1851-1900	4.388*	-0.107*	0.053	0.25
1901-1950	7.992*	-0.219*	0.167*	0.72
1951-1988	15.271*	-0.222*	-0.150	0.72

* $p < .05$
** $p < .01$
*** $p < .001$

Table 10.2

Associations Of Marriage And Birth Rates With Suicide Rates In Sweden

Pearson Correlations	birth	marriage
total suicide rate		
1776-1970	-0.84***	-0.48***
1776-1825	0.25	0.23
1826-1875	-0.49***	-0.67***
1876-1925	-0.48***	-0.41**
1926-1970	-0.57***	-0.64***
male suicide rate		
1776-1970	-0.79***	-0.52***
1776-1825	0.25	0.24
1826-1875	-0.48***	-0.67***
1876-1925	-0.41**	-0.44**
1926-1970	-0.67***	-0.71***
female suicide rate		
1776-1970	-0.87***	-0.33***
1776-1825	0.19	0.13
1826-1875	-0.35*	-0.45***
1876-1925	-0.64***	-0.22
1926-1970	-0.29*	-0.39*

Multiple Regressions

	constant	birth	marriage	R^2
total suicide rate				
1776-1970	23.45**	0.03	-0.11	0.96
1776-1825	4.85	0.01	0.04	0.78
1826-1875	17.67***	0.18	-0.92**	0.54
1876-1925	14.61	0.22	0.01	0.79
1926-1970	34.81***	0.01	-0.80*	0.74
male suicide rate				
1776-1970	31.71***	-0.04	-0.11	0.95
1776-1825	10.95*	-0.12	0.18	0.81
1826-1875	32.99***	0.34	-1.86**	0.49
1876-1925	29.39	0.35	-0.39	0.75
1926-1970	55.45***	-0.45	-0.91*	0.69
female suicide rate				
1776-1970	12.32*	0.07	-0.10	0.92
1776-1825	-0.29	0.11	-0.06	0.27
1826-1875	6.76**	0.03	-0.24	0.39
1876-1925	4.47	-0.08	0.37	0.63
1926-1970	18.03***	0.09	-0.53	0.76

* $p < .05$
** $p < .01$
*** $p < .001$

Table 10.3

Associations Of Marriage And Birth Rates With Suicide Rates In Switzerland

	birth	marriage		
Total Suicide Rate				
Pearson Correlations				
1876-1912	-0.13	-0.55***		
1913-1950	-0.25	0.34*		
1951-1988	-0.81***	-0.69***		
1876-1988	-0.09	-0.05		
Multiple Regressions	constant	birth	marriage	R^2
1876-1988	22.460***	0.171	-0.207	0.70
1876-1912	34.641***	0.045	-0.909*	0.29
1913-1950	11.153	1.094*	-0.384	0.53
1951-1988	30.293***	-1.107*	0.512	0.89

* $p < .05$
** $p < .01$
*** $p < .001$

Chapter Eleven

ALCOHOL USE, SUICIDE AND HOMICIDE

The association between alcohol use and abuse and suicide is well-documented (Lester, 1992) and goes both ways. Suicide individuals have high rates of alcohol use and abuse (e.g., Hawton, et al., 1989), and alcohol abusers have high rates of suicidal behavior (e.g., Wilhelmsen, et al., 1983). Alcohol use is also associated with homicide -- the majority of murderers are intoxicated at the time of the murder (Wolfgang, 1958). It seems likely that alcohol use and abuse weaken the individual's inhibitions against impulsive violence.

There are many micro-behavioral explanations for the association between alcohol use and abuse and suicide. Menninger (1938) viewed alcohol abuse as a manifestation of the self-destructive impulse, and he called alcoholism a form of chronic suicide. Kendall (1983) suggested four reasons for the association between alcohol abuse and suicide: (1) alcohol abuse may be a source of stress as a result of the social decline of individuals who abuse alcohol, (2) alcohol may result in psychological consequences, such as lower self-esteem and greater depression, which may increase the risk of suicide, (3) depression may be the primary etiological factor leading to both alcohol abuse and suicidal behavior, and (4) alcohol abuse may weaken the body's resistance to damage, resulting in self-destructive behavior having more lethal consequences.

At the macro-behavioral (aggregate) level, the association between suicide rates and alcohol use is supported by both cross-sectional and time-series studies. Suicide rates are found to be higher in regions where alcohol use and abuse are higher (Lester, 1989), and years with higher rates of alcohol consumption also have higher rates of suicide. For example, Skog and Elekes (1993) found that the time-series suicide rate in Hungary was strongly associated with the annual sales per capita of alcoholic beverages. However, as we have seen hitherto in this volume, results from studies conducted in one nation do not always generalize to other nations.

The present study was designed to explore the time-series association between alcohol use and rates of personal violence (suicide and homicide) in a set of nations with available data. Comparable data were available for thirteen nations (listed in Table 11.1) for suicide rates and nine nations (also listed in Table 11.1) for homicide rates. For suicide rates, the associations were also examined for males and females separately.

Data on alcohol consumption per capita in nations were available for 1950-1972 from the Finnish Foundation for Alcohol Studies (1977). An attempt was made to extend this period by using data from other sources (e.g., Adrian, 1984), but this was not possible owing to the lack of consistency between different data sources. For example, while Switzerland was given a consumption rate of 10.8 liters of absolute per capita for 1972 by both sources, the United States was given values of 6.8 by the Finnish Foundation and 7.2 by Adrian, whereas Czechoslovakia received values of 8.6 and 9.5 respectively.

Since divorce has been shown earlier in this book to be strongly associated with suicide and homicide rates in some nations, divorce rates were included in the analyses in order to see whether alcohol consumption contributed to the prediction of suicide and homicide rates above and beyond the impact of divorce rates. Thus, the independent variables were alcohol consumption and divorce rates, and the dependent variables were suicide and homicide rates. The time-series analyses were conducted as usual, with the statistical package provided by Doan (1990), using the Cochrane-Orcutt technique to correct for the serial autocorrelation in the data sets.

The results are shown in Tables 11.1 and 11.2. For suicide, it can be seen that, both in the regression analyses and the simple Pearson correlational analyses, suicide rates were positively associated with both alcohol use and divorce rates. In the correlational analyses, 10 of the 13 correlation coefficients were positive for alcohol use (binomial p = 0.046) and 11 for divorce rates (p = 0.011). In the regression analyses, nine of the 13 regression coefficients were positive both for alcohol use and for divorce rates. The majority of the coefficients which were statistically significant were positive.

For homicide rates, in both sets of analyses, eight of the nine coefficients were positive, both for alcohol use and for divorce rates. Again, the majority of the statistically significant coefficients were positive.

Looking at the data by gender (Table 11.2), it can be seen that the impact of alcohol consumption on suicide was positive and found for both genders in seven of the nine nations.

The results of this study indicate that, for many nations, in times when alcohol consumption is higher, suicide and homicide rates are also higher and, furthermore, the association between rates of personal violence and alcohol consumption was found even after divorce rates were taken into account by means of multiple regression analyses. However, the results also indicate that this association is not found in every nation. For example, in New Zealand and Switzerland, years with higher rates of alcohol consumption had lower suicide rates.

An alternative way of conceptualizing the variables used in this study is to view divorce, suicide and homicide as alternative modes of expressing psychological distress. Thus, alcohol may contribute to higher rates of one of these symptoms of distress in some nations and to the other symptoms in other nations. To explore this, the association between alcohol consumption and all three symptoms of distress (suicide, homicide and divorce) was examined using the present data sets. The results, shown in Table 11.3, indicate that alcohol consumption is positively associated with all three symptoms of distress (suicide, homicide and divorce) in the majority of nations, with the association found in more nations for suicide and divorce than for homicide.

The present results indicate again the importance of replicating research in several nations in order to check upon the reliability of the results. If the present study had been conducted only on Sweden, the association between alcohol consumption would have been confirmed; had it been conducted on New Zealand, the association would not have been confirmed. Yet the association was found in nine of the 13 nations studied.

These results lead to the next research question, namely, why is the association between alcohol use and rates of personal violence found in some nations, but not in others? Apparently, there exist some mediating factors which work to mitigate the impact of alcohol on personal violence. If we were able to identify social characteristics which differ in the nations where the association is found from those in the nations where the association is not found, our understanding of the connection between alcohol use and abuse and personal violence might improve.

REFERENCES

Adrian, M. International trends in alcohol production, trade and consumption, and their relationship to alcohol-related problems, 1970-1977. *Journal of Public Health Policy*, 1984, 5, 344-367.

Doan, T. A. *Regression analysis of time series*. Evanston, IL: Var Econometrics, 1990.

Hawton, K., Fagg, J., & McKeown, S. Alcoholism, alcohol and attempted suicide. *Alcohol & Alcoholism*, 1989, 24, 3-9.

Kendall, R. E. Alcohol and suicide. *Substance & Alcohol Actions/Misuse*, 1983, 4, 121-127.

Lester, D. Alcohol consumption and rates of personal violence (suicide and homicide). *Activitas Nervosa Superior*, 1989, 31, 248-251.

Lester, D. Alcoholism and drug abuse. In R. W. Maris, A. L. Berman, J. T. Maltsberger & R. I. Yufit (Eds.) *Assessment and prediction of suicide* (pp. 321-336). New York: Guilford, 1992.

Menninger, K. *Man against himself*. New York: Harcourt, Brace & World, 1938.

Skog, O. J., & Elekes, Z. Alcohol and 1950-1990 Hungarian suicide trend. *Acta Sociologica*, 1993, 36, 33-46.

Wilhelmsen, L., Elmfeldt, D., & Wedel, H. Causes of death in relation to social and alcohol problems among Swedish men aged 35-44 years. *Acta Medica Scandinavica*, 1983, 213, 263-268.

Wolfgang, M. E. *Patterns of criminal homicide*. Philadelphia: University of Pennsylvania, 1958.

Table 11.1
Alcohol Use And Rates Of Personal Violence, 1950-1972

	Correlations(r)		Regressions(b)		
	alcohol	divorce	alcohol	divorce	R^2
Suicide					
Belguim	0.76*	0.63*	0.97	-3.40	0.59
Canada	0.95*	0.96*	1.07*	1.91*	0.97
Czechoslovakia	0.92*	0.87*	1.27*	-0.62	0.85
Denmark	-0.11	0.52*	-1.61	7.12*	0.76
Finland	0.56*	0.52*	0.49	2.42	0.66
Luxembourg	0.37*	0.82*	-0.54	20.24*	0.71
Netherlands	0.79*	0.69*	0.21	1.56	0.74
New Zealand	-0.26	-0.01	-0.41	1.19	0.14
Norway	0.67*	0.64*	0.70	0.50	0.45
Sweden	0.86*	0.65*	4.13*	-8.06*	0.89
Switzerland	-0.85*	-0.03	-2.11*	8.01	0.81
USA	0.81*	0.74*	1.40*	-0.79	0.80
West Germany	0.66*	0.53*	0.14	2.16	0.67
Homicide					
Belgium	0.73*	0.77*	0.18*	-0.22	0.77
Canada	0.95*	0.93*	0.24	0.41*	0.94
Finland	0.23	0.23	0.26	0.20	0.40
Netherlands	0.88*	0.75*	0.06*	0.10	0.79
New Zealand	0.01	0.30	-0.10	0.67*	0.19
Norway	-0.42*	-0.12	0.05	0.04	0.72
Sweden	0.73*	0.70*	0.10	0.15	0.53
USA	0.99*	0.97*	1.69*	0.93*	0.98
West Germany	0.72*	0.74*	0.02*	0.49*	0.84

* significant at the 5% level or better

Table 11.2
Alcohol Use And Suicide Rates By Gender, 1950-1972
Regression Results

	men			women		
	alcohol	divorce	R^2	alcohol	divorce	R^2
Belgium	0.97	-6.19	0.27	1.14	-2.08	0.69
Canada	1.28*	2.50*	0.95	0.64*	1.45*	0.96
Denmark	-2.54*	9.50*	0.82	-0.45	4.57*	0.64
Finland	0.86	3.67	0.57	0.03	1.23	0.60
Netherlands	0.16	2.25	0.66	0.22	1.16	0.69
Norway	1.19	-1.93	0.26	0.02	3.84	0.49
Switzerland	3.37*	9.53*	0.82	-0.76*	4.80*	0.35
USA	0.35	0.02	0.25	2.76*	-1.96*	0.93
West Germany	0.14	2.11	0.37	0.34*	0.61	0.82

* significant at the 5% level or better

Table 11.3

The Association Between Alcohol Consumption And Symptoms Of Distress,
1950-1972

	Suicide		Homicide		Divorce	
	r	b	r	b	r	b
Belgium	0.76*	0.66*	0.73*	0.16*	0.94*	0.09*
Canada	0.95*	1.78*	0.95*	0.40*	0.90*	0.39*
Czechoslovakia	0.92*	1.17*	-	-	0.96*	0.18*
Denmark	-0.11	0.81	-	-	0.72*	0.36*
Finland	0.56*	1.06*	0.23	0.30	0.97*	0.24*
Luxembourg	0.37	0.80	-	-	0.65*	0.01
Netherlands	0.79*	0.37*	0.88*	0.07*	0.78*	0.14*
New Zealand	-0.26	-0.23	-0.01	0.01	0.61*	-0.01
Norway	0.67*	0.81*	-0.43*	0.06	0.92*	0.24*
Sweden	0.86*	2.05*	0.73*	0.13*	0.91*	0.07
Switzerland	-0.85*	-0.31	-	-	0.37	-0.03*
USA	0.81*	0.78*	0.99*	2.01*	0.96*	0.81*
West Germany	0.66*	0.30	0.72*	0.05*	0.32	0.10*

* significant at the 5% level or better

Chapter Twelve

SOCIAL INTEGRATION AND SUICIDE FROM 1901 TO 1988

In Chapter 2, we presented the results of time-series analyses of the social correlates of the suicide rate for 36 nations for the period 1950-1985. It is of interest to explore what the results would be if the period studied was extended. The present chapter explores the answer to this question.

The data available limit the number of nations which can be included in these analyses. Few nations have reported suicide rates for the Twentieth Century, and some nations did not report data on measures of social integration (such as marriage and birth rates) during the First and Second World Wars. Mitchell (1992) provided data for birth and marriage rates for 1901 to 1988 (but not divorce rates), and complete data for these two variables and for suicide rates were available for only twelve nations (which are listed in Table 12.1). The present analyses should be compared with those reported in Table 2.2 of Chapter 2 where regressions were run using the same variables for the period 1950-1985.

The time-series regressions were carried out as before using Doan's (1990) statistical package and the Cochrane-Orcutt technique to correct for serial autocorrelation.

Looking at the correlations, it appears that birth and marriage rates are both more often negatively associated with suicide rates than positively associated, in accordance with Durkheim's theory of suicide. Marriage and children should lead to greater social integration and so lower suicide rates. However, the ratio of negative to positive correlation coefficients is only 8 to 4 or 9 to 4, except for birth rates and suicide rates for females (where 11 of the 12 correlation coefficients are negative -- one-tailed binomial p = .003). However, in the multiple regressions, the coefficients are roughly split between positive and negative.

Despite the less consistent associations in these results (as compared to those in Chapter 2 for the period 1950-1985 -- see Table 2.2), the R^2 values are quite large, with a median of 0.84.

COMMENT

The present analyses for twelve nations during the Twentieth Century (1901-1988) have shown that the negative associations between measures of domestic social integration (marriage and birth rates) and suicide rates are not as consistent as those found for the later part of this century (1950-1985). Thus, it may be that alternative sociological theories of suicide may be needed to explain these long-term trends in suicide rates and that other social factors may need to be introduced into the equations.

REFERENCES

Doan, T. A. *Regression analysis of time series.* Evanston, IL: Var Econometrics, 1990.

Mitchell, B. R. *International historical statistics.* New York: Stockton Press, 1992.

Table 12.1
Domestic integration and suicide rates, 1901-1988

Correlations

	total		males		females	
	birth	marriage	birth	marriage	birth	marriage
Australia	0.02	-0.39*	0.18	-0.49*	-0.31*	0.03
England/Wales	0.04	0.18	0.31*	0.17	-0.43*	0.15
Finland	-0.90*	0.04	-0.88*	0.07	-0.91*	-0.04
Ireland#	-0.49*	0.01	-0.50*	-0.05	-0.40*	0.15
Italy	0.42*	0.05	0.48*	0.05	0.05	-0.01
Netherlands	-0.74*	-0.50*	-0.43*	-0.55*	-0.88*	-0.34
New Zealand	-0.32*	-0.19	-0.20	-0.07	-0.46*	-0.40*
Norway	-0.73*	-0.41*	-0.70*	-0.42*	-0.72*	-0.38*
Scotland	-0.65*	-0.16	-0.46*	-0.28*	-0.79*	0.08
Spain^	-0.38*	-0.26*	-0.30*	-0.27*	-0.54*	-0.25*
Sweden	-0.58*	-0.35*	-0.34*	-0.29*	-0.71*	-0.38*
Switzerland	-0.09	-0.02	0.22*	0.08	-0.71*	-0.19

The frontiers of Ireland changed during this period after Northern Ireland was split off.
^ Data were available for Spain only for the period 1901-1987.
* two-tailed $p < .05$ or better.

Regressions

	constant	birth	marriage	R^2
total				
Australia	8.52*	0.05	0.25	0.70
England/Wales	8.61*	0.08	0.01	0.88
Finland	25.80*	0.39*	-0.31*	0.93
Ireland#	6.96*	-0.16	0.05	0.87
Italy	6.01*	0.08	-0.03	0.86
Netherlands	10.86*	-0.21*	0.09	0.74

New Zealand	15.01*	-0.11	-0.17	0.52
Norway	71.68	0.01	-0.31*	0.91
Scotland	10.02*	-0.03	-0.03	0.89
Spain^	7.45*	-0.07	-0.03	0.71
Sweden	21.03*	-0.03	-0.25	0.78
Switzerland	19.65*	0.34	-0.18	0.73
Males				
Australia	12.40*	0.15	0.25	0.72
England/Wales	13.48*	0.09	0.08	0.88
Finland	42.66*	0.94*	-0.73*	0.93
Ireland#	11.69*	-0.28	0.01	0.84
Italy	8.62*	0.15*	-0.07	0.89
Netherlands	12.77*	-0.19*	0.10	0.61
New Zealand	19.01*	-0.12	0.04	0.66
Norway	21.69*	-0.06	-0.36	01.86
Scotland	13.62*	-0.02	-0.05	0.85
Spain^	11.46*	-0.11	-0.06	0.65
Sweden	31.04*	-0.06	-0.30	0.61
Switzerland	29.18*	0.61	-0.34	0.79
Females				
Australia	4.10	-0.01	0.21	0.84
England/Wales	4.99*	0.03	0.07*	0.93
Finland	9.07*	-0.15*	0.12	0.89
Ireland#	2.25	-0.08	0.12	0.74
Italy	3.55*	0.01	0.02	0.85
Netherlands	9.65*	-0.28*	0.09	0.83
New Zealand	10.01	-0.11*	-0.25*	0.27
Norway	8.27*	0.02	-0.24*	0.85
Scotland	6.75*	-0.08	0.01	0.85
Spain^	3.50*	-0.03	-0.02	0.73
Sweden	10.72*	0.03	-0.15	0.88
Switzerland	15.02	-0.34	0.15	0.71

Chapter Thirteen

STUDIES OF ETHNIC GROUPS WITHIN A NATION

Up to this point in this book, we have explored correlates of the time-series suicide rate of the general population in different nations. However, some nations are ethnically heterogeneous, and it is of interest to inquire whether the associations are similar for each ethnic group. The present chapter reports three studies on this issue from nations with heterogeneous populations: Singapore, the United States and South Africa.

SINGAPORE

Singapore has three major ethnic groups and a residual category: Chinese (76.4% of the population in 1990), Malay (14.9%), Indians (6.4%) and "others" (2.3%) (CIA, 1990). Suicide rates for Chinese, Malay and Indian and "other" residents of Singapore for 1955-1984 were obtained for Singapore with the help of Dr. S. C. Emmanuel (Ministry of Health) -- the data are shown in Table 13.1. As before, the association of these suicide rates with the overall Singapore marriage and birth rates was examined using the statistical package from Doan (1990), using the Cochrane-Orcutt technique to correct for the serial autocorrelation in the data sets.

The results are shown in Table 13.2. It can be seen that the pattern of correlations for the total population (a positive association between suicide rates and marriage rates and a negative association between suicide rates and birth rates was found only for the Chinese ethnic group. The associations for Malays, Indians and "Others" were different.

In the multiple regressions, the results for the four ethnic groups differed considerably, with only the patterns for Indians and "Others" resembling each other.

Thus, the present study has indicated that the trends identified in a multi-ethnic society may differ considerably for each ethnic group.

THE UNITED STATES

Black and white suicide rates for the United States were available for the period 1960-1990 from Lester (1998). Although birth rates by race were available for 1964-1990, marriage and divorce rates were not available by race. Accordingly, crude marriage, birth and divorce rates for the total population were used in the multiple regression analyses.

The results are shown in Table 13.3. It can be seen that the results were similar for both black and white Americans, with marriage and divorce rates correlating positively with suicide rates, while birth rates correlated negatively.

SOUTH AFRICA

In 1990, the population of South Africa was 73.8% black, 14.3% white, 9.1% colored and 2.8% Indian (CIA, 1990). It was possible to obtain marriage, birth and divorce rates *separately* for Whites, Coloreds and "Asians" -- rates for blacks were not available. Thus, the examination of the associations is more meaningful than for Singapore and the United States.

Suicide and homicide rates for Whites, Coloreds and Asians in South Africa for 1950-1985 were obtained with the help of Dr. Aubrey Levin,

Rhodes University and Fort England Hospital -- the rates are shown in Table 13.4. Marriage, birth and divorce rates were obtained for each ethnic group with the help of Mrs. I. E. van Reenen from the Central Statistical Service in Pretoria. The data sets were complete except for divorce rates for all three ethnic groups in 1963 and Asians in 1966; interpolation was used to estimate divorce rates for these missing data points. As before, the time-series multiple regressions were carried out with a statistical package from Doan (1990), using the Cochrane-Orcutt method to correct for the serial autocorrelation in the data sets.

The results are shown in Table 13.5. From the simple Pearson correlation coefficients, it can be seen that the strongest correlates of suicide rates were divorce rates for Whites and Asians, followed by birth rates, while birth rates were the strongest correlate for Coloreds. The statistically significant correlations were in the direction predicted by Durkheim's theory of suicide. In the multiple regressions, only the associations of suicide rates with divorce rates remained as statistically significant predictors of the suicide rate for Whites and Asians. The percentage of the variance in the suicide rate accounted for by the three social variables was 57% for Whites, 49% for Coloreds and 21% for Asians.

The results for homicide were slightly different but more consistent across ethnic groups. For all three groups, the Pearson correlations indicated a negative association of birth rates with homicide rates and a positive association of divorce rates with homicide rates. In the multiple regressions, divorce rates were the significant predictor of homicide rates for all three ethnic groups. The percentage of the variance in the homicide rates accounted for by the three social variables was 52% for Whites, 73% for Coloreds and 40% for Asians, higher in general than for suicide rates.

It appears, therefore, that measures of domestic integration are associated with the suicide rates of Whites, Coloreds and Asians in South Africa from 1950 to 1985, but the statistically significant predictors are different for Coloreds than for Whites and Asians. The significant associations are in accord with predictions from Durkheim's theory of suicide.

The associations of the measures of domestic integration with homicide rates were more consistent across ethnic groups than those for suicide rates but, in contrast to Henry and Short's prediction, were in the same direction as those for suicide. Thus, domestic integration appears to protect South Africans of all three ethnic group from both suicide and from homicide.

COMMENT

The results in this chapter have indicated that the associations between measures of domestic social integration and suicide rates may differ for each ethnic group within a society. Furthermore, the data for South Africa have indicated the usefulness of obtaining measures of social integration for each ethnic group separately.

REFERENCES

CIA. *World Factbook*. Washington, DC: US Government Printing Office, 1990.

Doan, T. A. *Regression analysis of time series*. Evanston, Illinois: Var Econometrics, 1990.

Lester, D. *Suicidal behavior in African Americans*. Commack, NY: Nova Science, 1998.

Table 13.1
Suicide rates by ethnic group in Singapore, 1955-1984

	Chinese	Indians	Malays	Others
1955	13.8	16.4	2.9	25.0
1956	11.8	20.6	1.1	56.0
1957	12.8	16.9	0.0	45.9
1958	10.3	12.4	1.5	17.6
1959	12.9	14.9	0.5	8.9
1960	10.8	8.7	2.2	7.9
1961	10.6	13.2	3.4	0.0
1962	11.4	5.6	1.2	14.0
1963	12.1	6.2	2.0	6.7
1964	10.5	6.0	1.6	19.9
1965	8.7	13.0	0.4	6.2
1966	11.5	14.0	0.7	9.3
1967	11.1	10.7	0.7	10.3
1968	13.3	11.8	1.7	5.0
1969	11.1	9.9	1.4	1.6
1970	10.1	12.9	0.6	11.5
1971	12.8	10.2	1.9	10.3
1972	12.5	16.7	1.2	5.0
1973	12.5	13.2	2.1	12.2
1974	11.2	22.8	0.9	2.4
1975	14.2	9.7	1.5	7.0
1976	14.3	8.9	1.7	9.0
1977	12.0	12.0	1.2	0.0
1978	12.9	14.4	1.4	4.3
1979	13.1	13.0	1.4	4.2
1980	13.5	19.4	1.4	3.9
1981	14.0	13.4	3.1	11.3
1982	14.1	19.0	2.2	7.4
1983	15.2	13.1	1.9	5.4
1984	14.6	17.8	2.7	12.3

Table 13.2
Correlations and regression results for four ethnic groups in Singapore, 1955-1984

	Total	Chinese	Malays	Indians	Others
Pearson Correlations					
marriage	0.39**	0.44**	0.10	0.27	-0.46
birth	-0.33*	-0.45**	-0.13	-0.09	0.61**
Multiple Regressions					
constant	6.62**	14.22**	2.23	-12.87	-61.98**
marriage	0.31*	0.04	-0.01	1.94**	3.75*
birth	0.03	-0.09	-0.03	0.47**	1.76**
R^2	0.24	0.35	0.08	0.29	0.54

* $p < .05$
** $p < .01$

Table 13.3
Correlations and regression results for black and white American suicide
rates, 1960-1990

	blacks	whites
Correlations		
marriage	0.56**	0.52**
birth	-0.84***	-0.84***
divorce	0.94***	0.91***
Regressions		
constant	6.36	18.61***
marriage	-0.31	-0.48**
birth	-0.05	-0.18*
divorce	0.82***	0.49***
R2	0.93	0.88

*   p < .05
** p < .01
*** p < .001

Table 13.4
Suicide and homicide rates by race in South Africa, 1950-1985

	Suicide			Homicide		
	white	colored	Asian	white	colored	Asian
1950	9.47	2.53	11.11	2.03	9.82	4.56
1951	14.05	1.63	7.34	3.02	9.67	4.35
1952	9.36	1.57	12.93	2.41	13.35	3.43
1953	11.95	2.87	9.72	2.95	15.02	4.86
1954	11.11	2.69	12.23	2.32	10.81	7.19
1955	11.37	2.29	12.23	2.32	10.80	7.19
1956	11.16	2.90	8.16	2.91	14.81	2.80
1957	11.56	2.73	9.77	3.27	14.46	5.45
1958	9.15	3.00	8.19	2.31	14.56	6.42
1959	12.09	2.97	6.05	3.82	13.66	3.46
1960	14.24	4.33	8.19	2.12	14.20	5.46
1961	17.15	3.80	9.22	2.44	13.90	2.87
1962	16.89	4.42	8.75	3.40	14.69	2.98
1963	16.77	15.39	7.35	3.70	15.57	5.42
1964	16.00	13.81	9.42	2.61	22.23	4.90
1965	16.08	13.58	8.58/	3.46	23.51	4.56
1966	14.09	12.53	8.66	3.52	27.17	4.77
1967	13.89	4.36	9.76	3.10	26.51	5.48
1968	13.87	4.43	7.32	3.26	24.77	6.16
1969	13.53	4.36	11.25	3.58	24.11	4.50
1970	12.42	3.18	9.66	2.38	26.22	4.45
1971	14.50	3.79	10.63	2.50	29.14	8.53
1972	12.42	3.93	8.35	0.88	10.33	1.61
1973	19.26	7.04	12.73	2.99	32.14	5.72
1974	16.94	8.75	15.38	2.43	35.80	6.01
1975	20.29	7.36	14.34	3.83	59.31	11.20
1976	15.41	4.78	8.54	3.42	46.68	9.08
1977	15.21	4.71	6.25	3.62	33.80	5.08
1978	15.82	4.73	5.73	3.86	26.02	4.45

1979	13.31	4.63	6.85	4.32	26.71	4.61
1980	22.91	8.46	42.37	4.07	57.44	35.53
1981	28.38	10.26	40.79	8.90	102.50	53.71
1982	18.48	5.22	7.29	6.65	80.08	15.28
1983	21.91	7.52	27.85	5.65	63.41	24.17
1984	21.49	4.85	10.72	5.78	55.82	9.93
1985	14.28	3.01	5.76	2.88	31.71	9.87

Table 13.5
Correlations and regression results for three ethnic groups in South Africa,
1950-1985

	Whites	Coloreds	Asians
		Suicide	
Pearson correlations:			
marriage	0.03	-0.53***	0.15
birth	-0.65***	-0.15	-0.28**
divorce	0.73***	0.13	0.39***
Multiple regressions:			
(b coefficients shown)			
constant	-8.07	13.48	-9.57
marriage	-0.21	-1.40	0.33
birth	0.61	0.03	0.43
divorce	5.79**	1.67	17.32*
R^2	0.57	0.49	0.21
		Homicide	
Pearson correlations:			
marriage	-0.02	0.01	0.17
birth	-0.60***	-0.73***	-0.47***
divorce	0.70***	0.81***	0.53***

Multiple regressions:
(b coefficients shown)

constant	-2.79	10.13	-4.15
marriage	-0.36	2.16	0.37
birth	0.24	-0.50	0.10
divorce	2.14***	45.20**	21.36*
R^2	0.52	0.73	0.40

* $p < .10$
** $p < .05$
*** $p < .01$

Chapter Fourteen

MEASUREMENT ISSUES: THE PROBLEM OF AGE

As we saw in Chapter 10 in the case of Sweden, occasionally nations report suicide rates based only upon the population 15 years of age and older. This makes good sense since it was customary for many years to never classify any death by someone under the age of 15 as suicide both because suicide was rare in those under the age of 15 and because it was difficult to determine suicidal intent in the deaths of child and young adolescents. In recent years, this restriction has begun to erode because cases of attempted and completed suicide in children and young adolescents have been documented and because such actions appear to be more common than hitherto. Nevertheless, it remains difficult for medical examiners and coroners to ascertain suicidal intent in these children and young adolescents because of the likelihood that their concept of death may not be mature. Thus, in most nations, the number of deaths recorded officially as suicides among those under the age of 15 is still miniscule.

Furthermore, since one of the measures of social integration used in the present analyses is the birth rate, the birth rate and suicide rate could be associated negatively simply based on a statistical artifact when the suicide rate is calculated on the basis of the total population: if the birth rate is high, more children are born, leading to a larger total population and, therefore, a lower suicide rate. This is called *negative collinearity* in regression analyses.

One way that nations have tried to deal with the problem of the varying age-structure of the population over time is to calculate "age-adjusted" suicide rates. The procedure is based on the keeping the age structure of the population constant, with a base year chosen for the age structure. The proportions of the population with different ages is applied to all future years. Thus, in subsequent years, the actual suicide rate is modified by assuming that the age-structure in the present year is the same as in the base year.

The analyses so far in this book have used crude suicide and homicide rates which have not been adjusted for the changing age structure of the nations over time. Some nations calculate and publish age-adjusted time-series suicide rates, and the present chapter explores whether the use of age-adjusted rates makes a great difference to the results. For the present book, age-adjusted suicide rates were obtained for four nations: Canada, France, Japan and the United States.

Taking into account both of these considerations, this chapter will explore briefly the impact of using suicide rates based on the population over the age of 15 rather than the total population. The only nation that provides suicide rates based on the population over the age of 15 is Israel, and so the first study examines predictors of the time-series suicide rate in Israel as compared to the United States. The second study compares the results of a time-series analysis in the United States using suicide rates based on the total population versus the population over the age of 15. The third study in this chapter explores the effect on the results of the time-series analyses if age-adjusted suicide rates are used instead of crude suicide rates.

ISRAEL VERSUS THE UNITED STATES

Data on Israeli suicide rates by gender for the Jewish population from 1960-1989 were available from Dr. Eitan Sabatello of the Israeli Central Bureau of Statistics. (The raw data are shown in Table 14.1.) For purposes of comparison, suicide rates by gender for the United States were calculated by the present authors for the same period based on the population over the age of 15 also (see Table 14.1). These suicide rates were correlated with the crude marriage, birth and divorce rates obtained as in Chapter 2 from the United Nations (annual). The results of a correlational and multiple regression analysis (again correcting for serial autocorrelation by means of the Cochrane-Orcutt technique) are shown in Table 14.2

Looking at the simple Pearson correlations, domestic social integration was not associated with male Israeli suicide rate for the correlation coefficients failed to reach statistical significance. However, domestic social integration was positively associated with Israeli female suicide rate. This indicates that Israeli women had higher suicide rates in years when marriage and birth rates were higher, and they had lower suicide rates in years when divorce rates were higher. This phenomenon is in conflict with predictions from Durkheim's modified theory of suicide and implies that the multiple roles held by Israeli females creates suicidogenic stress.

American male suicide rates conformed to Durkheim's modified theory as far as divorce and birth rates were concerned, while American female suicide rates were unrelated to measures of domestic social integration.

In the multiple regressions, the success of the predictions was better for Israeli female suicide rates than for Israeli male suicide rates (the R^2 for females was higher than that for males). For Israeli females, the regression coefficient for divorce rates remained negative and that for marriage positive. The coefficient for the birth rate was now negative for Israeli female suicide rates, however. Although the coefficients failed to reach statistical significance, the results of the regression do indicate that marriage may be deleterious to the mental health of Israeli women as indicated by their suicide rate, a suggestion made by Gove (1972) for American women. Suicide among Israeli women may be fatalistic/altruistic in nature, that is, the result of too much social integration/regulation rather than too little.

For American men and women, the results of the regressions indicated conformity to Durkheim's modified theory, and the regression coefficients were statistically significant for the American male suicide rates. Thus, multiple roles do not appear to pose as much conflict for American women as they do for Israeli women.

The more important issue, however, is whether the results *within* a nation depend upon whether suicide rates based on the total population or suicide rates based on the adult population are used. This issue is explored using data from the United States.

THE EFFECT OF CHANGING THE POPULATION BASE

Are the results of a time-series analysis different if the population base for calculating suicide rates is the population over the age of 15 rather than the total population? The present analysis explores the association of marriage, birth and divorce rates on the male and female suicide rates of the United States from 1960-1989 using suicide rates based on the total population and based on the population over the age of fifteen. The results are shown in Table 14.3.

It should be noted first of all that the suicide rates based only on the population over the age of 15 are, of course, much higher than those based on the total population. Since it is more meaningful to use rates based only on the adult population, American suicide rates are considerably higher than official government statistics would lead us to believe.

The Pearson correlations between the two types of suicide rates were 0.93 for males and 0.91 for females, indicating strong associations. However, the associations with the measures of domestic social integration did differ somewhat. The associations using the rates based on the population over the age of 15 were, on the whole, smaller, and fewer were statistically significant.

The results of the regressions, in contrast, showed few differences, and the R^2 values were not consistently better for one type of suicide rate than the other. Furthermore, the signs of all of the regression coefficients were in the direction of supporting Durkheim's modified theory of suicide, with marriage and birth rates protecting against suicide and divorce rates increasing the suicide rate.

THE EFFECT OF USING AGE-ADJUSTED RATES

As mentioned in the introduction to this chapter, the third set of analyses in this chapter compares the results of time-series analyses using crude and age-adjusted suicide rates.

Age-adjusted suicide rates were available for Canada for 1950-1985, France for 1950-1985, Japan for 1953-1986, and the United States for 1950-

1985. The results for crude and age-adjusted suicide rates are shown in Table 14.4, which shows simple correlation coefficients for both sets of rates and the results of the multiple regressions (with corrections for the serial autocorrelation in the data sets).

It can be seen that the results changed very little after the switch from crude suicide rates to age-adjusted suicide rates. Occasionally, the level of statistical significance changed (for example, the role of divorce rates on Japanese male suicide rates), and the R^2 value shifted a small amount. However, the pattern of results remained similar for both crude and age-adjusted suicide rates. This highlights the fact that, for the purpose of explaining the time-series variation in the suicide rate of a nation, the choice of whether to use crude suicide rates or age-adjusted suicide rates does not seem to matter greatly.

It should be noted, however, that the changes in the size of the crude and age-adjusted coefficients did sometimes reach statistical significance. For example, for the Japanese data, all of the Pearson correlation coefficients based on crude suicide rates differed significantly from those based on age-adjusted suicide rates. In addition, the association of divorce rates with the male suicide rate differed greatly in the two sets of analyses.

COMMENT

The present analysis, therefore, has indicated that suicide rates based on the adult population may usefully be employed in time-series analysis. Furthermore, at least for the United States, the results using suicide rates based on the total population and on the adult population do differ a little, especially in the simple correlational analyses. On the other hand, the use of age-adjusted rates made little difference to the results for three of the four nations studied, but their impact on the results should be considered in future time-series research.

REFERENCES

Gove, W. Sex, marital status and suicide. *Journal of Health & Social Behavior*, 1972, 13, 204-213.

United Nations. *Demographic yearbook*. New York: United Nations, annual.

Table 14.1
Suicide Rates

based on	Israel# population > 15		United States* population > 15		United States# total population	
	male	female	male	female	male	female
1960	15.0	13.3	24.2	7.1	16.5	4.9
1961	14.9	13.5	23.8	7.0	16.1	4.9
1962	12.1	12.1	24.3	7.8	16.5	5.4
1963	12.7	10.0	24.3	8.3	16.5	5.8
1964	12.7	10.1	23.7	8.0	16.1	5.6
1965	12.4	7.9	23.9	8.6	16.3	6.1
1966	11.9	7.9	23.5	8.3	16.1	5.9
1967	13.9	10.1	22.9	8.5	15.7	6.1
1968	15.9	12.4	22.9	8.2	15.8	5.9
1969	16.5	11.0	22.9	8.7	16.1	6.3
1970	12.4	9.4	23.5	9.0	16.7	6.5
1971	13.4	11.5	23.4	9.3	16.7	6.8
1972	13.9	12.0	24.2	9.1	17.5	6.8
1973	10.9	7.9	24.2	8.7	17.7	6.5
1974	14.5	8.5	24.4	8.6	18.1	6.5
1975	17.0	10.0	25.3	8.9	18.9	6.8
1976	14.9	8.6	24.7	8.6	18.7	6.7
1977	15.9	7.8	26.1	8.7	20.1	6.8
1978	13.5	8.3	24.7	8.0	19.0	6.3
1979	14.9	7.8	24.3	7.7	18.6	6.0
1980	15.0	7.3	24.3	7.0	18.6	5.4
1981	13.3	7.2	24.4	7.3	18.7	5.8
1982	10.2	6.3	25.1	7.0	19.2	5.6
1983	13.7	6.6	25.0	6.9	19.2	5.4
1984	12.5	5.8	25.7	6.9	19.7	5.4
1985	12.7	5.6	25.9	6.5	19.9	5.1
1986	14.0	7.6	26.8	6.8	20.6	5.4
1987	16.0	6.3	26.6	6.6	20.5	5.2
1988	15.9	6.6	26.1	6.3	20.2	5.0
1989	18.0	7.6	25.9	6.1	19.9	4.8

Suicide rates published by the governments
* Suicide rates calculated by the present authors

Table 14.2
Domestic social integration and suicide rates in Israel and the United States,
1960-1989

Pearson correlations			
	divorce rate	marriage rate	birth rate
Israeli males	0.19	0.03	-0.10
Israeli females	-0.63***	0.39*	0.50**
American males	0.65***	0.04	-0.44*
American females	-0.32	0.18	-0.01

Regressions					
	constant	divorce rate	marriage rate	birth rate	R^2
Israeli males	14.41	4.64	2.59*	-1.02	0.35
Israeli female	19.70	-6.83	1.55	-0.67	0.70
American males	34.89***	0.83*	-1.15**	-0.13	0.79
American females	-23.58	0.16	-0.29	-0.21	0.86

* two-tailed $p < .05$
** two-tailed $p < .01$
*** two-tailed $< .001$

Table 14.3
Domestic social integration in America using suicide rates based on the total
population and on the adult population, 1960-1989

Correlations					
		marriage rates	birth rates	divorce rates	
Rates based on total population:					
male		0.32	-0.67***	0.87***	
female		0.47**	-0.39*	0.09	
Rates based on population > 15:					
male		0.04	-0.44*	0.65***	
female		0.18	-0.01	-0.32	
Regressions					
	constant	marriage	birth	divorce	R^2
Rates based on total population:					
male	24.03***	-1.05**	-0.08	1.46***	0.92
female	-11.50	-0.23	-0.16	0.35	0.81
Rates based on population > 15:					
male	35.02***	-1.16**	-0.13	0.84*	0.79
female	-23.58	-0.29	-0.21	0.16	0.86

* two-tailed p < .05
** two-tailed p < .01
*** two-tailed < .001

Table 14.4
Correlates Of Crude And Age-Adjusted Suicide Rates[5]

| | Correlations | | Regressions | |
	crude suicide rates	age-adjusted suicide rates	crude suicide rates	age-adjusted suicide rates
Canada: Total				
divorce	0.97*	0.92*	1.784*	0.975*
marriage	0.07	0.11	0.148	0.244
birth	-0.93*	-0.96*	-0.201*	-0.277*
crude suicide rate		0.99*		
R^2			0.98	0.96
Canada: Male				
divorce	0.98*	0.94*	3.040*	1.867*
marriage	-0.01	-0.01	-0.268	-0.212
birth	-0.90*	-0.93*	-0.222*	-0.304*
crude suicide rate		0.99*		
R^2			0.97	0.95
Canada: Female				
divorce	0.87*	0.79*	0.626*	0.456
marriage	0.26	0.32	0.552*	0.695*
birth	-0.94*	-0.93*	-0.154*	-0.145*
crude suicide rate		0.99*		
R^2			0.96	0.95
France: Males				
divorce	0.80*	0.74*	6.04*	5.43*
marriage	-0.91*	-0.89*	-2.16*	-2.27*
birth	-0.48*	-0.40*	0.84*	0.92*
crude suicide rate		0.99*		

[5] The regression coefficient for the constant is omitted

R^2				0.94	0.91
France: Females					
divorce	0.94*	0.93*		3.86*	3.57*
marriage	-0.82*	-0.80*		-0.13	-0.11
birth	-0.81*	-0.84*		0.16	0.13
crude suicide rate		1.00*			
R^2				0.95	0.95
Japan: Males					
unemployment	0.79*	0.67*		4.512*	4.018*
change in gnp	-0.17	-0.02		-0.078	-0.067
female labor force	0.60*	0.76*		0.872*	0.831*
divorce	-0.10	-0.31*		2.088	-2.258
crude suicide rate		0.97*			
R^2				0.93	0.95
Japan: Females					
unemployment	0.47*	0.36*		1.635	1.643*
change in gnp	0.07	0.20		-0.024	-0.026
female labor force	0.75*	0.87*		0.345	0.387
divorce	-0.45*	-0.61*		-4.725	-6.471
crude suicide rate			0.97*		
R^2				0.90	0.95
The United States					
divorce	0.90*	0.76*		0.43*	-0.07
marriage	0.56*	0.48*		-0.37*	-0.33*
unemployment	0.49*	0.43*		-0.01	0.06
birth	-0.90*	-0.90*		-0.15*	-0.23*
crude suicide rate		0.94*			
R^2				0.92	0.89

* statistically significant at the .05 level or better

Chapter Fifteen

SEGMENTING THE POPULATION BY GENDER AND AGE

Chapter 2 illustrated that measures of domestic integration (that is, marriage, birth and divorce rates) were quite successful in predicting the time-series suicide rates of nations. It is of interest next to explore the effect of segmenting the population by gender and age. Specifically, we attempted to explore whether these measures of domestic integration are equally useful in predicting the time-series suicide rates of males aged 15-24, males aged 25-34.......females aged 15-24, etc.

The time-series suicide rates for the different segments of the population are more difficult to obtain than the overall suicide rate. Accordingly, it was necessary to restrict the time period to 1960-1990 and, even so, data were available for only 20 nations: Australia, Austria, Belgium, Canada, Denmark, Finland, France, Greece, Hungary, Israel, Japan, the Netherlands, New Zealand, Norway, Portugal, Sweden, Switzerland, West Germany, the United States and Yugoslavia.[6] The suicide rates for these nations by gender and age are shown in Appendix D.

---

[6] Data were also available for Ireland, Italy and Singapore, but these nations did not permit divorce for some years during the period. In addition, although data were

In addition, the size of the data set increases enormously, as well as the tables of results. Therefore, a summary of the correlation and regression results, rather than complete tables of data for each nation, will be presented in this chapter.

Based on Durkheim's theory of suicide, the predictions are for a positive association between suicide and divorce rates and negative associations between suicide and marriage rates and between suicide and birth rates. Thus, for each nation, the association will either have the predicted sign or not. In this 20-nation sample, two categories will result: if the proportion of the nations with the expected sign is P, then the proportion with the other sign will be (1-P).

The probability of obtaining x nations with the predicted sign and N-x with the other sign follows the binomial distribution which is given by

$$p(x) = {}_NC_x \, P^x \, (1\text{-}P)^{N\text{-}x}$$

where P is proportion expected to have the predicted sign under the null hypothesis. Two-tailed tests of statistical significance were used in order to be conservative. In order to get a statistically significant deviation from the expected distribution under chance (P = 0.5), 15 or more nations or 5 or fewer nations out of 20 are the critical values for rejecting the null hypothesis using two-tailed tests (Siegel, 1956, p. 250).

The results of the 840 Pearson correlation coefficients and 840 regression coefficients are presented in Table 15.1, where for each nation the number of coefficients in the predicted direction is shown in for each of the three measures of domestic integration.

It can be seen that the results expected on the basis of Durkheim's theory of suicide (that is, negative associations for birth and marriage rates with suicide rates and a positive association for divorce rates with suicide rates) was found most clearly for males aged 15-24, 25-34 and 35-44. Only four other significant trends were noted: a negative association between divorce and suicide rates for males aged 55-64 and a positive association for females aged 75+, a negative association between marriage and suicide rates for males

---

available for England/Wales, Scotland and Northern Ireland, measures of domestic integration were not available for all three regions of the United Kingdom for the full period.

aged 75+, and a negative association between birth and suicide rates for females aged 15-24; three of the four trends are in a direction opposite to that predicted by Durkheim's theory.

Looking at the regression coefficients, only the positive association between divorce and suicide rates for males 15-24, 25-34 and 35-44 remained statistically significant.

The conclusion is that the associations between measures of domestic integration (birth, marriage and divorce rates) reported in Chapter 2 are found primarily for the suicide rates of men aged 15-44 and that the association is strongest and most stable for divorce and suicide rates. Even so, the association for this limited group (men aged 15-44) is not found in every nation. Thus, it appears that Durkheim's theory of suicide applies best to young men and that alternative theories may be required to explain the time-series variation in modern suicide rates for older men and for women of all ages.

REFERENCE

Siegel, S. *Nonparametric statistics for the behavioral sciences.* New York: McGraw-Hill, 1956.

Table 15.1
The number of negative correlations and regression coefficients for each sex-
by-age group, 1960-1990

Pearson Correlations			
	birth	marriage	divorce
males, 15-24	18*	15*	4*
males, 25-34	20*	19*	3*
males, 35-44	17*	15*	5*
males, 45-54	12	11	10
males, 55-64	6	9	15*
males, 65-74#	9	10	8
males, 75+#	13	15*	6
females, 15-24	16*	13	6
females, 25-34	14	12	6
females, 35-44	12	12	6
females, 45-54	12	11	9
females, 55-64	10	11	12
females, 65-74	13	13	6
females, 75+	13	12	4*
Regression Coefficients			
(Cochrane-Orcutt technique)			
males, 15-24	11	11	2*
males, 25-34	11	15*	3*
males, 35-44	12	12	4*
males, 45-54	10	11	7
males, 55-64	7	9	10
males, 65-74 #	7	9	6
males, 75+ #	10	12	4*
females, 15-24	14	8	8
females, 25-34	14	12	8
females, 35-44	9	10	8
females, 45-54	9	12	8
females, 55-64	13	19	10
females, 65-74	7	10	8
females, 75+	13	6	9

only 19 coefficients were available for these groups since Yugoslavia did not break down elderly suicide rates into these two categories

Chapter Sixteen

A STUDY OF SMALLER REGIONS

So far in this book, we have examined the predictors of the time-series suicide rates of nations as a whole. It is of interest to inquire whether similar associations would be found for the time-series suicide rate of smaller regions within a nation. The present chapter reports the results of a study of the states of America from 1960-1988, with the exception of three states which do not report divorce rates consistently (Indiana, Louisiana and New Mexico).

The results of the Pearson correlations and the multiple regressions (using the Cochrane-Orcutt technique to correct for the serial autocorrelation in the data sets) are shown in Table 16.1.

It can be seen that the most consistent Pearson correlations were between divorce and suicide rates (83% positive) and between birth and suicide rates (91% negative). The consistent associations of suicide rates with divorce and birth rates (positive and negative, respectively) were in accord with Durkheim's theory of suicide. The association of suicide rates with marriage rates (60% positive), however, was not. In America, the positive association between suicide and marriage rates may be a result of the high divorce rate, which means that many marriages are, in fact, remarriages of those who have been divorced. Thus, a high marriage rate in America may be in part due to a high divorce rate.

For the regressions, all three trends were significant: between divorce and suicide rates (79% positive), between birth and suicide rates (85% negative), and between marriage and suicide rates (83% negative), all in the direction predicted by Durkheim's theory of suicide.

In the regression analyses, only Alabama and Kansas had all three regression coefficients statistically significant (incidentally, with coefficients consistent with Durkheim's theory of suicide). A look at the R^2 values shows that they range from 0.05 (for Wyoming) to 0.87 (for Oklahoma), indicating that there must be other social and economic factors at work in determining the time-series suicide rates in the states and that these factors may differ from state to state. The size of the regression coefficients may reflect in part the magnitude of the variables in the states, but also the relative importance of the three social variables in determining the suicide rates of the states.

From these analyses, we can conclude that measures of domestic integration and suicide rates are strongly associated over time in the states of America in recent years. The associations were not found in every state, although the trends were clear over all of the 47 states with available data.

Table 16.1
Associations of suicide rates with marriage, birth and divorce rates for the
states of America, 1960-1988

Pearson Correlations

	marriage	divorce	birth
AK	-0.07	0.01	-0.09
AL	0.16	0.72*	-0.81*
AR#	0.84*	0.69*	-0.74*
AZ	0.76*	0.75*	-0.75*
CA	-0.34	-0.03	-0.22
CO	0.28	0.59*	-0.61*
CT	-0.45*	-0.44*	0.38*
DE	0.31	0.44*	-0.48*
FL	0.78*	0.90*	-0.88*
GA	-0.06	0.84*	-0.81*
HI	0.10	0.49*	-0.17
IA	-0.37*	-0.01	0.02
ID	-0.51*	0.55*	-0.43*
IL	-0.72*	0.16	-0.15
KS	0.27	0.41*	-0.42*
KY	0.42*	0.87*	-0.81*
MA	0.33	0.71*	-0.61*
MD	-0.32	0.25	-0.25
ME	0.08	0.19	-0.12
MI	0.12	0.88*	-0.86*
MN	0.21	0.58*	-0.46*
MO	-0.13	0.36*	-0.27
MS	0.03	0.84*	-0.81*
MT	0.09	0.44*	-0.32
NC	0.08	0.82*	-0.81*
ND	0.22	0.53*	-0.29
NE	-0.27	0.09	-0.07
NH	-0.21	0.09	-0.10
NJ	-0.38*	-0.26	0.37*

NV	-0.28	-0.45*	-0.49*
NY	-0.74*	-0.22	0.23
OH	0.84*	0.84*	-0.74*
OK	0.06	0.92*	-0.63*
OR	0.64*	0.59*	-0.73*
PA	0.46*	0.90*	-0.77*
RI	0.39*	0.86*	-0.76*
SC	-0.01	0.80*	-0.84*
SD	-0.26	0.66*	-0.26
TN	0.79*	0.89*	-0.83*
TX	0.68*	0.89*	-0.77*
UT	0.62*	0.82*	-0.10
VA	0.53*	0.64*	-0.73*
VT	0.07	0.30	-0.23
WA	-0.10	-0.07	-0.12
WI	0.63*	0.79*	-0.67*
WV	-0.12	0.60*	-0.45*
WY	-0.10	-0.05	-0.12

Regressions

	marriage	divorce	birth	R^2
AK	-0.048	-0.074	-0.164	0.09
AL	-0.316*	0.319*	-0.239*	0.79
AR#	0.864*	0.274	-0.061	0.79
AZ	0.530	0.508	-0.207	0.66
CA	-0.537	0.406	-0.309	0.78
CO	-0.348	0.403*	-0.114	0.40
CT	-0.404	-0.244	-0.031	0.26
DE	-0.178	0.062	-0.229	0.25
FL	-0.175	0.541	-0.340	0.83
GA	0.018	0.718	-0.054	0.72
HI	-0.154	1.232*	0.297	0.41
IA	-0.907*	0.474	-0.069	0.31
ID	-0.212	0.530	-0.215	0.39
IL	-0.679*	-0.221	-0.170	0.62
KS	-0.564*	0.489*	-0.193*	0.30

KY#	-0.113	0.914*	-0.063	0.77
MA	-0.267	0.888*	0.038	0.54
MD	-0.401	-0.670	-0.100	0.13
ME	0.027	1.117	0.419	0.12
MI	-0.009	0.459	-0.173	0.79
MN	-1.045*	1.011*	-0.035	0.52
MO	-1.709	1.025	-0.351	0.72
MS	-0.405	0.976*	-0.140	0.80
MT	-1.563*	2.008*	-0.195	0.52
NC	-0.102	0.218	-0.246	0.72
ND	-0.116	0.776*	0.007	0.28
NE	-0.315	-0.044	-0.088	0.16
NH	-0.647*	-1.273	-0.432	0.15
NJ	-0.346	0.245	0.120	0.24
NV	0.008	-0.132	-0.330	0.27
NY	-1.064*	0.146	-0.056	0.67
OH	0.629	0.483	0.146	0.77
OK	-0.147	1.688*	-0.068	0.87
OR	-0.398	0.278	-0.556*	0.57
PA	-0.223	1.053*	-0.032	0.84
RI	-1.581*	1.825*	-0.200	0.81
SC	0.164	0.581	-0.278	0.73
SD	-0.272*	1.071*	-0.132	0.56
TN	0.045	0.780*	0.041	0.76
TX	-0.263	1.312*	-0.050	0.84
UT	-0.005	1.460*	-0.129	0.68
VA	-0.937	-0.303	-0.588*	0.67
VT	-0.531	0.524	-0.007	0.11
WA	-0.141	-0.334	-0.220	0.15
WI	-0.522	0.886*	-0.127	0.65
WV	-0.341	0.796*	-0.016	0.61
WY	-0.086	-0.018	-0.118	0.05

* statistically significant at the 5% level or better
# interpolation for one year of divorce rates. IN, LA and NM could not be included because of extensive missing divorce data.

Chapter Seventeen

CONCLUSIONS

This book has presented the most comprehensive set of time-series analyses of national suicide and homicide rates ever produced. Efforts were made to collect suicide and homicide rates from as many nations as possible, resulting in a compilation of data sets for 36 nations. The statistics published by the World Health Organization served as the foundation of the data sets, but these statistics had many missing data points. The authors, therefore, wrote to government offices in many nations and to suicidologists in those nations in order to locate data for those years. Occasionally, nations appeared to have lost their data for those years, with no chance of ever recovering them. In other cases, government officials and scholars were able to provide the missing data. We would like to thank all of those who helped us in this task.

The time span for the majority of the data sets was 36 years (from 1950 to 1985). For a smaller subset of 20 countries, suicide rates by gender and age were compiled for 1960 to 1990. Finally, for three countries (Finland, Sweden and Switzerland) suicide rates back into the Eighteenth and Nineteenth Centuries were obtained.

The analyses tested primarily the role of social integration and regulation to predict these time-series suicide and homicide rates, and so were based on Durkheim's (1897) classic sociological theory of suicide. On the whole, Durkheim's theory performed remarkable well, which attests to Durkheim's genius and vision. For example, in Chapter 2, time-series analyses of suicide rates from 1950 to 1985 for 29 nations showed that the majority of the nations experienced a positive association between suicide and divorce rates and a negative association between suicide and marriage rates. Thus, as Durkheim predicted, suicide rates rose for these nations along with the divorce rate but declined with the marriage rate over the post-World War II period (1950-1985).

Second, the empirical results also indicated that the regression analyses provided more consistent confirmation of Durkheim's theory than did the Pearson correlational analyses. This was a surprising result since we had no *a priori* bias in favor of regression analyses over simple correlation analyses.

The next step for future researchers is to explain the deviations, that is, why did seven of the 29 nations experience a negative association between suicide and divorce rates while 22 conformed to Durkheim's prediction? Are there Durkheimian and non-Durkheimian societies and, if so, why?

Third, the time-series analyses also indicated that Durkheim's theory of suicide may have some usefulness for explaining the time series homicide rate, although the theory may require modification in order to perform as well as it does for suicide rates. In contrast, Henry and Short's (1954) proposal that suicide and homicide would show opposite associations with social indicators was not supported by the present series of analyses.

Fourth, more detailed analyses indicated that the success of Durkheim's theory of suicide depends, not only on the particular nation under study, but also upon sex, age, ethnic group and era. Furthermore, modern eras conformed better to Durkheim's theory than previous centuries.

Fifth, we also explored the association of other social indicators, such as unemployment and alcohol consumption, with suicide and homicide rates and showed that they too may play a significant role in explaining the time-series variation in suicide and homicide rates. Both of these social indicators may be by-products of modern society, suggesting that modernization may play a role in increasing suicide, and perhaps homicide, rates.

Lastly, two major issues in this research were illustrated nicely by the present analyses: the importance of cross-national generality and the difference between ecological and time-series results.

CROSS-NATIONAL GENERALITY

Many studies have been, and continue to be, published in which trends in suicide and homicide are explored in one nation. Although such analyses may play an important informational role in the nation, they have little interest for scholars until the generality of the results are shown. For instance, the fact that suicide rates are rising in young males in one nation has little interest for scholars of suicide until it can be determined that this trend is found in most nations. Thus, the implications of such trends depend critically upon whether the trend is found in most nations or only in a few nations.

Consequently, scholars must make every effort to replicate their findings from one nation in other nations. Only then will we make progress in identifying and testing general theories of suicide.

ECOLOGICAL VERSUS TIME-SERIES RESEARCH

In Chapter 1, we discussed the issue of whether different theories are required to explain ecological and time-series sociological research since often the results from the two types of research differ.

In the present case, Durkheim's theory of suicide performed quite well in explaining the time series suicide rates of nations, as well in fact as it did in explaining the ecological variation in suicide rates over the states of America (Lester, 1994) and over nations of the world (Lester, 1996).

Despite this congruence, a more detailed examination of the results by age and sex reveals several inconsistencies[7], and so it is important to explore these inconsistencies in future research in order to see whether they do require modification of existing theories or development of new theories.

Firebaugh (1980) noted that such inconsistencies (between ecological and time-series analyses) should not be viewed as the result of sampling error, measurement error or aggregation bias. Rather, scholars should consider the possibility that the underlying causal mechanisms differ.

---

[7] For example, male versus female differences in the results are much greater for the time-series studies than for the ecological studies.

Firebaugh noted that the results from the two types of studies can differ for several reasons. For example, cross-sectional studies measure long-run, cumulative effects whereas time-series studies tap short-run adjustments. In addition, they omit different variables from the analyses[8]. To look at the differences from another perspective, when cross-sectional international data are studied, each observation represents one nation in a given year. This observation captures, as it were, the phenomenon of suicide in a snapshot and at the same time explores the effects of the static social and political environment on suicide. In contrast, time-series data document the dynamic process as one snapshot leads to the next.

Figure 18.1
Hypothetical relationship between suicide and fertility
(adapted from Firebaugh, 1980)

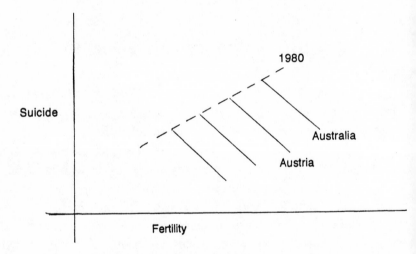

To illustrate the way in which opposite results can be obtained from ecological and time-series analyses, a hypothetical example (adapted from Firebaugh [1980]) is shown in Figure 18.1. For each nation over time, a negative association between fertility and suicide is shown, with the

---

[8] For example, in cross-sectional studies of homicide in the states of the United States, the "southernness" of the states is often used as a social variable, but it is not possible to include this variable in time-series analyses since measures over time of this variable are not possible.

regression lines for Australia and Austria marked. However, for a given year, such as 1980, the data for each nation could be such that the ecological association between fertility and suicide was positive, as indicated by the broken line in Figure 18.1.

Firebaugh argued that "[d]etermining which [type of analysis] is more appropriate is a theoretical question, not a methodological one.....In short, the question of whether to use [ecological] or [time-series] methods in a comparative study must be determined ultimately by theoretical considerations, not by methodological fiat" (p. 342). Thus, suicidologists need to give much more thought to their theories of suicide in order to see which type of methodology is appropriate for their theory.[9]

Finally, we should note that we used relatively simple multiple regression techniques in the present set of studies. More advanced econometric techniques are available, and future research should explore the results of using these techniques.[10]

REFERENCES

Durkheim, E. *Le suicide*. Paris: Felix Alcan, 1897.

Firebaugh, G. Cross-national versus historical regression models. *Comparative Social Research*, 1980, 3, 333-344.

Henry, A. F., & Short, J. F. *Suicide and homicide*. New York: Free Press, 1954.

---

[9] For example, at the individual level, does the theory propose (or assume) that people compare their condition with the condition of those in neighboring regions or with their own condition in previous years?

[10] For example, Yang (1994) explored whether the time-series suicide rate can be viewed as a random walk.

Lester, D. *Patterns of suicide and homicide in America.* Commack, NY: Nova Science, 1994.

Lester, D. *Patterns of suicide and homicide in the world.* Commack, NY: Nova Science, 1996.

Yang, B. A random walk hypothesis for Durkheim's theory of suicide. In D. Lester (Ed.) *Emile Durkheim: Le Suicide one hundred years later.* Philadelphia: Charles Press, 1994, 319-324.

Appendix A

SUICIDE AND HOMICIDE RATES 1950-1985

Suicide Rates

	Australia	Austria	Belgium	Canada	Chile	Costa Rica	Czech	Denmark
1950	9.3	23.8	12.9	7.8	4.2	2.3	18.3	23.3
1951	9.6	22.7	13.8	7.4	4.6	2.5	17.7	23.6
1952	10.6	22.7	13.1	7.3	-	2.6	18.4	22.9
1953	10.9	23.4	13.5	7.1	4.3	2.6	19.4	24.1
1954	10.8	23.1	13.8	7.2	4.4	3.2	19.8	23.3
1955	10.3	23.4	13.6	7.0	4.8	3.2	19.2	23.3
1956	10.8	22.8	14.6	7.6	7.4	2.6	19.9	22.5
1957	12.1	23.9	14.8	7.5	7.7	2.6	20.3	22.1
1958	12.3	23.3	14.9	7.4	6.8	2.7	20.1	21.2
1959	11.1	24.8	13.1	7.4	5.8	2.3	21.6	21.0
1960	10.6	23.0	14.6	7.6	7.4	2.1	22.3	20.3
1961	11.9	21.8	14.7	7.5	7.8	2.7	20.6	16.9
1962	13.7	22.4	13.6	7.2	6.6	2.4	20.6	19.0
1963	15.7	21.7	14.0	7.6	3.5	3.7	21.3	19.1
1964	14.6	22.8	14.0	8.2	3.0	3.0	20.6	21.0

1965	14.8	22.8	15.0	8.7	5.5	2.2	21.5	19.3
1966	14.0	23.1	14.4	8.6	6.7	3.2	23.0	17.8
1967	15.1	22.4	15.0	9.0	7.6	3.1	23.8	17.5
1968	12.7	21.9	15.5	9.7	8.1	2.7	24.5	20.5
1969	12.2	22.3	15.2	10.9	6.8	3.1	23.2	20.8
1970	12.4	24.2	16.5	11.3	6.0	2.3	25.3	21.5
1971	13.4	22.7	15.4	11.9	5.7	3.0	24.2	24.8
1972	12.3	23.4	15.6	12.2	5.5	3.3	24.7	23.9
1973	11.4	22.1	14.9	12.6	4.7	2.6	22.4	23.8
1974	11.5	23.7	15.6	12.9	5.5	4.2	22.9	26.0
1975	11.1	24.1	16.2	12.3	6.7	4.1	21.9	24.1
1976	10.8	22.7	16.6	12.8	5.6	5.7	20.8	23.9
1977	11.1	24.3	19.1	14.2	5.8	4.4	21.3	24.3
1978	11.2	24.8	20.5	14.8	5.2	4.1	21.4	23.3
1979	11.6	25.1	21.5	14.2	5.9	3.4	19.8	25.8
1980	11.0	25.7	22.1	14.0	4.9	5.4	20.0	31.6
1981	11.2	27.1	21.9	14.0	5.8	4.3	19.8	30.0
1982	11.7	27.6	21.9	14.3	5.6	3.9	19.9	29.0
1983	11.2	27.0	22.8	15.1	5.7	5.5	19.2	28.6
1984	11.0	26.9	23.8	13.7	6.2	4.5	18.5	28.7
1985	11.5	27.7	23.1	12.8	5.7	4.9	18.9	27.7

Suicide Rates

	Eng/ Wales	Finland	France	Hungary	Iceland	Ireland	Italy	Japan
1950	10.2	15.6	15.	22.2	11.9	2.6	6.5	19.6
1951	10.1	15.7	15.1	23.4	12.4	2.6	6.8	18.2
1952	9.8	17.6	15.5	25.3	11.5	2.2	6.3	18.4
1953	10.7	17.4	15.4	20.8	7.9	2.3	6.6	20.4
1954	11.3	18.9	16.2	17.7	12.3	2.0	6.1	23.4
1955	11.2	20.0	15.9	20.5	14.6	2.3	6.7	25.2
1956	11.8	22.4	17.4	19.4	12.4	2.6	6.8	24.5
1957	11.8	21.9	16.5	21.7	8.5	2.5	6.6	24.3
1958	11.7	21.3	16.6	23.4	5.3	2.7	6.3	25.7
1959	11.4	20.0	16.8	26.3	6.4	2.5	6.4	22.7
1960	11.1	20.5	15.8	26.0	7.4	3.0	6.3	21.6
1961	11.2	20.6	15.8	25.3	10.6	3.2	5.6	19.6
1962	11.9	22.1	15.1	25.2	9.3	1.8	5.5	17.6
1963	12.1	19.2	15.5	27.0	8.1	2.5	5.3	16.1
1964	11.7	19.8	14.9	28.7	9.5	2.0	5.5	15.1
1965	10.8	20.0	15.0	29.8	11.4	1.8	5.4	14.7
1966	10.4	19.5	15.5	29.8	18.9	2.4	5.1	15.2
1967	9.7	20.6	15.5	30.8	15.6	2.5	5.4	14.2
1968	9.4	21.9	15.3	33.7	7.5	2.4	5.4	14.5
1969	8.8	23.7	15.8	33.1	9.9	1.8	5.5	14.4
1970	8.0	21.3	15.4	34.6	13.2	1.8	5.7	15.2
1971	8.1	21.7	15.4	35.7	5.3	2.7	6.0	15.6
1972	7.7	24.0	16.1	37.0	8.6	3.0	5.8	17.0
1973	7.8	23.5	15.5	36.8	13.2	3.4	5.7	17.4
1974	7.9	25.1	15.6	41.1	10.2	3.8	5.4	17.5
1975	7.5	25.0	15.8	38.1	10.1	4.7	5.6	17.9
1976	7.8	25.8	15.8	40.6	8.6	5.7	5.7	17.6
1977	8.0	25.8	16.5	40.3	10.4	4.6	6.2	17.9
1978	8.2	25.2	17.2	43.1	11.6	4.9	6.4	17.6
1979	8.5	24.7	18.7	44.5	13.3	5.7	7.0	18.0

1980	8.8	25.7	19.4	44.9	10.5	6.3	7.3	17.7
1981	8.9	23.9	19.6	45.6	6.9	6.5	6.9	17.1
1982	8.6	24.1	20.9	43.5	9.4	6.9	7.4	17.5
1983	8.6	24.4	21.8	45.9	16.9	8.0	7.6	20.9
1984	8.7	25.2	22.0	46.0	18.4	6.6	6.1	20.4
1985	8.8	24.6	22.7	44.0	13.3	7.8	8.3	19.4

Suicide Rates

	Liech.	Luxem.	Mauritius	Mexico	Nether.	NZ	N Ireland	Norway
1950	14.5	14.5	6.5	1.8	5.5	9.2	3.5	7.4
1951	0.0	11.1	7.2	1.8	6.0	9.9	4.1	6.5
1952	7.0	11.0	5.4	2.4	6.3	10.1	3.0	6.9
1953	6.9	8.9	5.2	1.8	6.5	9.9	3.3	7.6
1954	20.5	10.5	6.6	1.5	6.2	8.9	3.5	7.4
1955	0.0	7.2	9.1	1.7	6.0	8.9	3.3	7.4
1956	33.0	9.8	6.7	1.6	6.0	9.1	3.9	7.3
1957	12.9	8.4	5.9	1.5	6.4	9.6	3.6	7.4
1958	2.7	9.3	5.4	1.5	6.8	9.6	3.1	7.3
1959	6.1	9.9	5.4	1.6	7.0	8.8	4.1	7.9
1960	6.0	10.2	3.1	1.5	6.6	9.7	4.4	6.5
1961	1.7	9.4	3.5	1.6	6.7	8.4	5.0	6.6
1962	11.3	9.3	2.2	1.6	6.6	8.4	4.2	7.9
1963	0.0	-	2.1	1.6	6.2	9.6	6.0	8.0
1964	0.0	10.6	2.9	1.5	6.5	8.0	5.4	7.3
1965	10.4	9.6	3.5	1.6	6.9	9.1	4.8	7.7
1966	25.1	17.3	3.8	1.5	7.1	9.2	5.5	7.1
1967	14.7	13.4	2.5	1.7	6.2	10.0	6.6	7.0
1968	0.0	12.5	2.3	1.6	6.3	9.6	6.6	8.1
1969	4.8	15.4	1.3	1.6	7.4	10.0	6.1	8.2
1970	18.7	14.1	1.7	1.5	8.1	9.6	3.9	8.4
1971	32.0	14.0	4.0	1.6	8.3	8.3	3.4	8.1
1972	17.8	15.0	2.3	1.4	8.2	8.8	3.0	9.0
1973	25.9	13.4	6.2	1.4	8.7	8.8	4.6	8.7
1974	12.6	13.0	4.5	1.5	9.2	9.0	4.1	10.4
1975	12.5	10.6	7.8	1.5	8.9	9.5	3.7	9.9
1976	4.1	14.4	6.5	1.5	9.4	9.3	4.5	10.8
1977	12.1	16.0	6.4	1.5	9.2	11.8	4.6	11.4
1978	15.8	18.5	7.7	1.5	9.7	10.3	4.6	11.7
1979	7.7	20.1	7.1	1.5	10.4	9.7	5.0	12.1

1980	11.9	12.9	2.5	1.0	10.1	10.8	5.3	12.4
1981	7.6	16.7	2.0	1.3	10.0	10.1	5.8	12.8
1982	3.8	21.3	1.4	1.4	10.7	11.4	6.0	14.0
1983	22.6	22.2	1.9	1.3	12.0	10.9	9.2	14.6
1984	11.2	18.9	12.1	1.5	12.4	11.9	7.0	14.5
1985	7.3	15.0	10.6	1.3	11.3	10.3	7.5	14.1

Suicide Rates

	Portugal	Puerto Rico	Scotland	Singapore	Spain	Sweden	Switzerland	Taiwan
1950	10.1	17.0	5.3	14.4	5.4	14.9	23.5	13.0
1951	10.1	14.4	5.4	9.0	5.9	16.2	21.1	16.0
1952	-	12.3	5.5	11.1	5.9	16.7	21.5	12.4
1953	-	11.5	5.5	13.3	5.9	18.6	21.8	13.8
1954	-	13.7	5.9	9.6	-	17.0	22.6	14.3
1955	9.2	11.3	7.7	10.7	5.5	17.8	21.6	15.5
1956	10.1	12.8	7.8	9.5	5.3	20.1	21.6	14.7
1957	8.1	11.3	8.2	10.2	5.3	19.9	20.9	13.7
1958	8.8	9.4	8.5	8.0	-	17.3	21.1	11.6
1959	9.2	10.9	8.5	10.6	5.2	18.1	19.4	15.1
1960	8.5	10.7	7.9	8.6	5.5	17.4	19.0	15.3
1961	9.0	10.3	7.9	8.5	5.2	16.9	18.2	16.4
1962	8.5	9.7	9.1	7.9	4.9	18.5	18.5	17.7
1963	9.5	10.0	8.6	8.6	4.9	18.5	16.8	18.1
1964	9.5	10.6	8.2	8.0	4.9	19.8	16.7	18.7
1965	9.2	12.3	8.0	7.7	4.7	18.9	18.4	16.5
1966	9.6	12.8	8.0	10.0	4.6	20.1	18.4	15.4
1967	9.9	9.6	7.5	9.4	4.4	21.6	17.6	13.5
1968	9.4	9.6	7.2	11.1	4.3	21.5	17.2	3.0
1969	8.6	10.3	7.0	9.2	4.4	22.0	17.4	13.1
1970	8.1	9.2	7.6	8.9	4.2	22.3	18.6	12.4
1971	8.1	9.8	7.2	10.9	4.3	20.3	18.6	10.8
1972	7.9	10.1	8.1	10.9	4.4	20.3	19.5	11.2
1973	8.2	9.4	8.4	10.9	4.2	20.8	18.8	10.2
1974	8.2	8.1	8.4	10.3	4.0	20.1	20.6	9.4
1975	8.3	8.2	8.2	11.1	3.9	19.4	22.5	9.6
1976	8.5	9.4	8.3	11.2	4.1	18.9	22.1	8.8
1977	8.9	10.2	8.1	9.6	4.1	19.7	23.9	9.6
1978	9.2	10.9	8.5	11.3	4.1	19.0	24.1	9.9
1979	9.7	8.7	9.6	10.4	4.1	20.5	24.7	9.9

1980	7.4	9.1	10.0	11.2	4.4	19.4	25.7	10.0
1981	7.9	9.3	10.0	7.8	4.6	17.5	23.8	11.3
1982	8.4	9.1	10.9	9.7	4.9	19.4	24.6	12.3
1983	9.8	9.9	9.8	10.7	5.7	19.0	25.2	12.0
1984	10.2	9.0	10.1	8.3	6.5	19.5	24.8	10.9
1985	9.7	8.0	11.1	12.8	6.5	18.2	25.0	11.9

Suicide Rates   Homicide Rates

	USA	West Germ	Yugoslav	Australia	Belgium	Canada	Eng/ Wales
1950	11.4	18.8	10.2	1.04	0.98	1.0	0.49
1951	10.4	19.2	8.8	1.35	0.94	1.1	0.42
1952	10.0	17.6	10.3	1.47	0.69	1.1	0.44
1953	10.1	18.3	10.0	1.30	0.59	1.2	0.41
1954	10.1	19.3	10.8	1.30	0.67	1.2	0.45
1955	10.2	19.3	11.1	1.40	0.69	1.1	0.42
1956	10.0	18.7	10.5	1.33	0.70	1.2	0.41
1957	9.8	18.3	11.3	1.32	0.64	1.1	0.54
1958	10.7	18.9	11.0	1.52	0.59	1.2	0.47
1959	10.6	18.7	12.0	1.48	0.64	1.0	0.54
1960	10.6	18.8	12.0	1.47	0.64	1.4	0.50
1961	10.4	18.7	11.9	1.35	0.72	1.2	0.55
1962	10.9	17.6	13.1	1.54	0.57	1.4	0.56
1963	11.0	18.5	12.8	1.36	0.64	1.3	0.54
1964	10.8	19.2	12.4	1.51	0.57	1.3	0.56
1965	11.1	20.0	12.4	1.43	0.75	1.3	0.58
1966	10.9	20.5	12.2	1.33	0.73	1.3	0.69
1967	10.8	21.3	12.8	1.38	0.75	1.6	0.67
1968	10.7	20.6	13.1	1.58	0.82	1.6	0.71
1969	11.1	20.9	13.9	1.25	0.84	1.8	0.66
1970	11.6	21.3	13.5	1.52	1.10	2.0	0.71
1971	11.7	20.9	13.7	1.76	1.01	2.2	0.82
1972	12.0	19.9	13.7	1.66	1.22	2.3	0.78
1973	12.0	20.8	13.1	1.89	1.09	2.4	0.90
1974	12.1	21.0	13.1	1.78	1.03	2.5	0.98
1975	12.7	20.9	13.5	1.63	0.91	2.7	0.99
1976	12.5	21.7	14.2	2.03	0.93	2.4	1.09
1977	13.3	22.7	14.6	1.92	0.89	2.6	0.91
1978	12.5	22.2	14.0	1.78	1.02	2.5	1.24
1979	12.1	21.5	14.1	1.84	1.60	2.5	1.06

1980	11.9	20.9	14.7	1.92	1.40	2.1	0.81
1981	12.0	21.7	15.7	1.89	1.30	2.3	0.35
1982	12.2	21.3	16.1	1.90	1.50	2.4	0.70
1983	12.1	21.3	16.1	1.91	1.74	2.4	0.64
1984	12.4	20.5	16.5	1.92	1.62	2.3	0.69
1985	12.3	20.7	16.0	1.99	2.03	2.1	0.69

Homicide Rates

	Finland	France	Hungary	Iceland	Ireland	Japan	Nether-lands	New Zealand
1950	2.9	0.7	2.84	0.7	0.30	2.26	0.32	1.05
1951	2.9	0.5	2.82	0.0	0.13	-	0.31	1.23
1952	3.0	0.6	1.87	0.7	0.23	2.03	0.28	1.00
1953	2.9	0.6	1.75	3.3	0.44	1.99	0.22	0.83
1954	3.0	0.6	2.07	0.0	0.14	2.19	0.25	0.86
1955	2.4	0.7	1.98	0.6	0.24	2.34	0.24	1.08
1956	2.4	0.8	28.15	0.0	0.10	2.03	0.16	0.51
1957	2.3	1.9	4.22	1.2	0.28	1.98	0.29	0.67
1958	2.1	2.2	2.58	0.6	0.21	2.13	0.32	1.05
1959	1.7	1.9	2.80	0.6	0.31	1.98	0.33	1.07
1960	2.6	1.6	1.57	0.0	0.10	1.84	0.30	1.01
1961	2.4	2.2	2.13	0.6	0.35	1.69	0.34	1.03
1962	2.6	1.5	1.94	0.0	0.10	1.54	0.23	0.77
1963	2.3	0.8	1.74	0.5	0.14	1.53	0.37	0.59
1964	2.0	0.8	1.71	0.5	0.21	1.52	0.37	0.89
1965	1.8	0.8	1.56	0.5	0.24	1.43	0.31	1.10
1966	2.2	0.7	1.87	0.5	0.24	1.42	0.41	0.75
1967	2.1	0.9	1.88	0.5	0.27	1.38	0.44	1.36
1968	2.1	0.8	2.28	1.5	0.34	1.45	0.39	0.73
1969	2.7	0.8	2.93	0.0	0.21	1.38	0.51	1.12
1970	2.1	0.7	2.68	0.0	0.37	1.32	0.48	1.21
1971	2.8	0.8	2.80	1.0	0.33	1.32	0.56	0.88
1972	3.3	0.9	2.71	0.0	0.62	1.30	0.53	1.03
1973	2.8	0.8	3.14	2.4	0.68	1.29	0.60	1.15
1974	2.6	0.9	2.89	2.3	1.63	1.27	0.81	1.46
1975	3.7	1.0	3.30	0.5	0.71	1.28	0.69	1.01
1976	3.3	0.9	3.40	1.8	0.59	1.26	0.81	1.06
1977	2.8	1.0	2.79	1.4	0.80	1.21	0.82	1.76
1978	3.0	1.0	2.45	1.3	0.70	1.14	0.80	1.86
1979	2.6	1.1	2.64	2.2	0.85	1.03	0.83	1.58

1980	3.3	1.0	2.96	1.3	0.70	0.96	0.78	1.41
1981	2.7	1.0	3.00	1.3	2.00	0.98	0.81	1.34
1982	2.8	1.1	2.84	0.0	0.65	0.93	0.85	1.30
1983	3.1	1.3	2.98	0.8	0.80	0.97	0.94	1.59
1984	2.7	1.3	3.30	0.4	0.55	0.95	0.95	1.18
1985	2.7	1.3	3.13	1.2	0.65	0.85	0.87	2.03

Homicide Rates

	N Ireland	Norway	Puerto Rico	Scotland	Sweden	USA	West Germany	Yugoslavia
1950	0.15	1.4	12.0	0.6	0.64	5.3	1.02	5.39
1951	0.29	1.1	8.0	0.4	0.61	4.9	1.09	5.41
1952	0.36	1.2	6.7	0.4	0.67	5.2	0.94	4.64
1953	0.58	1.2	7.0	0.7	0.66	4.8	1.01	4.46
1954	0.43	1.2	7.5	0.5	0.78	4.8	1.00	4.67
1955	0.36	0.9	7.4	0.5	0.66	4.5	1.06	4.45
1956	0.36	0.4	6.4	0.4	0.89	4.6	0.95	3.60
1957	0.64	0.5	5.4	0.6	0.73	4.5	0.93	3.51
1958	0.43	0.5	6.0	1.0	0.69	4.5	0.95	3.94
1959	0.28	0.5	6.0	0.5	0.70	4.6	0.98	4.00
1960	0.77	0.4	7.1	0.7	0.60	4.7	0.91	3.59
1961	0.56	0.4	7.5	0.4	0.52	4.7	1.03	3.45
1962	0.49	0.5	8.5	1.0	0.52	4.8	0.99	3.48
1963	0.28	0.7	7.8	0.7	0.83	4.9	1.03	3.48
1964	0.27	0.5	9.1	1.0	0.81	5.1	1.07	2.94
1965	0.07	0.5	8.6	1.1	0.72	5.5	1.13	3.07
1966	0.47	0.4	7.7	1.1	0.83	5.9	1.15	3.33
1967	0.54	0.4	7.4	1.2	0.89	6.8	1.22	3.47
1968	0.47	0.6	7.7	1.2	0.68	7.3	1.07	3.90
1969	0.66	0.7	8.3	1.5	0.89	7.7	1.24	3.39
1970	1.25	0.6	8.7	0.9	0.82	8.3	1.37	3.36
1971	0.84	0.6	12.3	1.3	0.94	9.1	1.31	3.72
1972	3.57	0.7	12.3	1.4	1.06	9.4	1.33	3.63
1973	10.13	0.8	14.9	1.4	1.00	9.8	1.21	2.96
1974	13.69	0.6	18.5	1.2	1.25	10.2	1.15	2.86
1975	11.49	0.7	17.1	1.5	1.15	10.0	1.21	2.58
1976	13.26	0.7	14.8	1.9	1.24	9.1	1.26	2.69
1977	14.18	0.8	15.7	1.9	1.16	9.2	1.17	2.40
1978	5.51	0.7	15.5	1.5	0.98	9.4	1.20	2.26
1979	4.38	0.9	15.3	1.5	1.35	10.0	1.10	2.16

1980	4.24	1.1	15.1	1.6	1.17	10.7	1.15	1.74
1981	7.28	1.3	16.7	1.6	1.43	10.3	1.27	2.26
1982	6.24	1.0	15.7	1.5	1.20	9.6	1.25	2.17
1983	6.16	1.2	13.0	1.6	1.21	8.6	1.20	1.96
1984	5.29	1.1	14.3	1.6	1.10	8.4	1.24	1.92
1985	3.72	0.9	17.1	1.3	1.23	8.3	1.18	1.73

SUICIDE RATES BY GENDER 1950-1985

	Australia		Austria		Belgium		Canada		Costa Rica		Denmark	
	m	f	m	f	m	f	m	f	m	f	m	f
1950	13.8	4.8	34.2	14.7	19.3	6.7	11.9	3.5	4.3	0.2	31.7	15.0
1951	14.3	4.7	32.4	14.2	20.4	7.5	11.1	3.6	3.9	1.2	32.1	15.1
1952	15.9	5.3	30.6	15.9	20.1	6.4	11.1	3.4	4.4	0.7	31.4	14.5
1953	15.6	6.0	32.7	15.3	19.7	7.4	11.0	3.2	4.8	0.4	32.3	16.0
1954	15.9	5.5	33.1	14.4	20.5	7.3	10.9	3.5	4.8	1.5	31.4	15.4
1955	15.1	5.4	33.1	15.1	19.9	7.3	10.7	3.4	5.9	0.4	32.0	14.8
1956	15.7	5.8	32.6	14.5	20.8	8.6	11.7	3.5	5.0	0.2	30.2	14.9
1957	17.3	6.9	34.4	15.1	21.0	8.6	11.7	3.3	5.2	0.0	29.7	14.6
1958	18.3	6.1	33.3	14.9	21.6	8.3	11.8	3.0	4.4	0.9	29.1	13.4
1959	16.3	5.8	36.0	15.3	18.8	7.5	11.5	3.1	4.2	0.4	28.7	13.5
1960	15.0	6.2	32.7	14.8	21.3	8.0	12.0	3.0	3.9	0.3	27.2	13.6
1961	16.9	6.7	31.3	13.6	21.7	7.9	11.9	3.0	5.0	0.3	22.4	11.5
1962	18.7	8.9	32.9	13.2	19.8	7.5	11.2	3.1	3.9	0.8	24.9	13.2
1963	20.7	10.6	31.0	13.4	19.4	8.7	11.4	3.8	6.1	1.3	25.7	12.6
1964	19.0	9.9	33.2	13.7	20.0	8.1	12.3	4.1	4.9	1.0	26.8	15.3
1965	18.7	10.8	32.0	14.7	20.6	9.6	12.9	4.5	3.9	0.4	24.0	14.7
1966	17.4	10.5	32.9	14.5	20.2	8.7	12.8	4.3	5.6	0.6	23.4	12.3
1967	18.9	11.1	32.6	13.4	20.8	9.3	13.2	4.8	5.7	0.5	23.6	11.6
1968	16.9	8.5	32.3	12.8	21.2	10.0	14.2	5.2	4.8	0.6	26.5	14.6
1969	16.6	7.8	31.3	14.4	21.3	9.3	15.6	6.2	5.8	0.5	26.6	15.2
1970	17.1	7.6	35.5	14.2	21.9	11.3	16.2	6.4	4.1	0.6	27.4	15.7

1971	17.5	9.0	31.7	14.7	21.5	9.5	17.3	6.4	5.4	0.7	31.5	18.1
1972	16.2	8.2	33.3	14.5	21.3	10.1	17.2	6.9	5.2	1.3	30.2	17.7
1973	15.3	7.3	31.6	13.6	20.7	9.3	18.0	7.1	4.0	1.2	29.2	18.5
1974	15.6	7.2	34.0	14.5	21.3	10.1	18.7	7.1	6.9	1.6	33.7	18.5
1975	15.1	6.9	35.5	13.9	21.0	11.5	17.8	6.8	6.2	1.9	29.9	18.4
1976	15.6	5.8	33.1	13.4	22.1	11.4	18.4	7.2	9.3	2.1	30.2	17.7
1977	15.9	6.2	34.8	14.9	24.9	13.4	21.2	7.3	6.6	2.1	30.9	17.8
1978	15.7	6.5	36.5	14.3	27.3	14.0	22.4	7.3	6.5	1.7	28.0	18.7
1979	16.5	6.6	36.7	14.7	28.2	15.0	21.4	7.0	5.7	1.1	31.8	19.8
1980	16.3	5.5	37.8	14.9	28.4	15.9	21.3	6.8	8.6	2.2	41.1	22.3
1981	16.9	5.5	40.4	15.1	29.0	14.6	21.3	6.8	6.8	1.8	38.9	21.3
1982	17.4	6.0	42.1	14.5	29.7	13.9	22.3	6.4	6.1	1.6	37.1	21.2
1983	17.0	5.4	40.0	15.4	30.3	16.3	23.4	6.9	9.5	1.6	37.0	20.4
1984	16.8	5.2	40.3	14.7	32.8	15.5	21.4	6.1	7.4	1.5	36.5	21.0
1985	18.2	5.1	40.9	15.7	31.6	15.0	20.5	5.4	8.6	1.2	35.1	20.6

Suicide Rates

	Eng/Wales		Finland		France		Hungary		Ireland		Italy	
	m	f	m	f	m	f	m	f	m	f	m	f
1950	13.5	7.0	26.7	5.4	23.8	7.2	32.5	12.6	4.2	0.9	9.5	3.6
1951	13.4	6.7	26.4	5.9	24.0	7.6	34.5	13.1	4.0	1.1	10.3	3.5
1952	13.2	6.8	30.0	6.3	24.0	7.4	36.2	15.2	3.5	0.9	9.3	3.6
1953	14.2	7.6	8.5	7.3	24.0	7.2	29.5	12.8	3.3	1.2	9.2	3.9
1954	14.9	8.1	31.2	7.6	24.7	7.4	24.6	11.3	3.2	0.8	8.7	3.6
1955	14.3	8.4	32.4	8.5	24.7	7.8	28.6	13.1	3.7	1.0	9.6	3.7
1956	14.9	9.0	37.0	9.0	26.4	9.0	27.9	11.8	4.4	0.8	9.7	3.8
1957	14.6	9.2	34.9	9.9	24.7	8.8	31.2	13.0	4.0	1.0	9.3	3.8
1958	14.6	9.1	33.9	9.7	24.9	8.8	33.2	14.4	4.2	1.2	8.8	3.6
1959	14.2	8.9	31.9	8.9	25.1	8.9	37.6	14.6	3.8	1.2	8.9	3.6
1960	13.8	8.7	32.9	9.0	24.0	8.2	35.6	14.9	4.1	1.8	8.7	3.7
1961	13.5	9.1	33.2	9.0	24.5	7.7	36.3	15.3	4.9	1.4	7.9	3.4
1962	14.4	9.7	35.2	9.9	23.2	7.5	35.6	14.9	2.9	0.8	7.8	3.2
1963	14.5	9.9	31.3	8.0	23.8	7.7	37.5	16.8	3.7	1.2	7.4	3.2
1964	13.8	9.8	30.9	9.5	22.4	7.8	40.9	17.1	3.4	0.7	7.7	3.2
1965	12.7	9.0	32.2	8.1	23.0	7.5	42.6	17.9	3.0	0.5	7.8	3.1
1966	12.1	8.8	30.0	9.1	23.3	8.1	42.0	18.0	3.6	1.2	7.3	3.0
1967	11.7	8.0	32.3	8.5	23.3	8.0	45.1	18.4	3.7	1.2	7.8	3.2
1968	11.4	7.6	34.6	9.5	22.5	8.4	49.1	19.3	3.8	1.0	7.6	3.1
1969	10.6	7.2	37.4	10.1	23.4	8.5	48.3	18.9	2.6	1.0	7.6	3.3
1970	9.5	6.6	34.4	9.2	22.8	8.4	50.8	19.8	3.0	0.5	8.1	3.5
1971	9.5	6.7	35.1	9.3	22.4	8.7	52.0	21.0	3.9	1.5	8.4	3.7
1972	9.2	6.2	39.0	10.0	23.3	9.3	53.4	21.4	4.3	1.7	8.2	3.6
1973	9.4	6.2	37.6	10.3	22.6	8.7	53.2	21.5	5.0	1.9	8.1	3.4
1974	9.5	6.4	40.6	10.5	22.7	8.8	58.9	23.6	5.9	1.7	7.3	3.5
1975	9.1	6.0	40.6	10.4	22.9	9.0	55.8	22.1	6.6	2.8	7.8	3.4
1976	9.7	5.9	42.3	10.3	22.9	9.0	57.9	24.3	7.9	3.4	7.9	3.5
1977	9.9	6.3	42.0	10.6	23.3	9.9	56.0	25.5	6.0	3.3	8.9	3.7
1978	10.2	6.3	41.9	9.7	24.7	10.0	60.4	26.9	6.4	3.5	9.3	3.8
1979	10.7	6.5	40.6	9.8	27.1	10.6	63.7	26.6	8.6	2.9	9.8	4.3
1980	11.0	6.7	41.6	10.7	28.0	11.1	64.5	26.5	8.3	4.3	10.1	4.6
1981	11.4	6.5	38.9	9.6	28.5	11.1	63.5	28.7	9.1	3.8	9.8	4.0
1982	11.5	5.9	38.5	10.6	30.4	11.8	62.0	26.2	10.2	3.6	10.7	4.4
1983	11.6	5.8	39.8	9.9	31.7	12.3	66.8	26.4	11.5	4.6	11.0	4.3
1984	11.8	5.7	41.4	10.0	32.2	12.4	67.6	25.7	9.2	3.9	11.3	4.5
1985	12.1	5.7	40.4	9.8	33.1	12.7	67.0	23.2	12.2	3.4	12.2	4.7

Suicide Rates

	Japan		Luxembourg		Nether.		N. Zealand		N Ireland		Norway	
	m	f	m	f	m	f	m	f	m	f	m	f
1950	24.1	15.3	21.5	7.4	7.4	3.7	13.4	4.9	5.3	1.7	12.4	2.6
1951	21.8	14.8	17.3	4.7	7.9	4.1	14.8	5.0	5.5	2.7	10.2	2.8
1952	21.8	15.1	16.6	5.3	8.2	4.4	15.0	5.1	4.5	1.6	10.3	3.5
1953	24.4	16.4	12.5	5.3	8.5	4.6	14.0	5.7	4.7	2.0	11.0	4.3
1954	29.1	17.8	15.1	5.8	8.2	4.3	13.4	4.4	5.3	1.7	12.2	2.7
1955	31.5	19.0	9.9	4.5	7.5	4.6	12.6	4.8	5.4	1.3	11.7	3.3
1956	29.8	19.4	17.1	2.6	7.1	4.9	12.0	6.2	4.8	2.9	11.8	2.8
1957	29.7	19.1	13.7	3.2	7.3	5.5	13.6	5.6	4.6	2.6	11.7	3.0
1958	30.7	20.8	13.6	5.1	8.5	5.1	14.3	4.9	4.5	1.7	11.8	2.8
1959	26.6	18.9	14.2	5.7	8.6	5.4	13.4	4.0	5.0	3.3	11.7	4.0
1960	25.1	18.2	16.7	3.8	8.2	5.1	13.8	5.5	5.8	3.0	10.4	2.5
1961	22.3	16.9	12.7	6.2	8.6	4.7	12.8	4.1	6.8	3.4	10.6	2.8
1962	20.4	14.8	13.8	4.9	8.0	5.3	11.3	5.3	5.1	3.4	12.6	3.2
1963	18.9	13.4	-	-	7.9	4.5	12.3	6.9	8.7	3.5	11.8	4.2
1964	17.5	12.9	11.1	10.2	8.2	4.9	9.7	6.2	6.9	4.0	11.4	3.2
1965	17.3	12.2	12.6	6.6	8.5	5.3	12.1	6.1	5.9	3.7	11.8	3.6
1966	17.4	13.1	25.2	9.4	8.9	5.3	11.6	6.7	6.5	4.6	10.6	3.6
1967	16.2	12.2	17.6	9.4	7.9	4.5	14.0	6.1	8.8	4.5	10.6	3.5
1968	16.5	12.5	20.0	5.3	8.0	4.7	13.0	6.2	7.0	6.2	12.1	4.1
1969	16.4	12.7	22.9	8.1	9.1	5.6	13.0	7.0	7.3	4.9	13.0	3.3
1970	17.3	13.3	21.0	7.5	9.9	6.2	12.6	6.6	4.7	3.2	11.8	5.0
1971	17.9	13.3	22.4	5.7	9.8	6.7	10.4	6.1	4.5	2.4	12.3	4.0
1972	19.7	14.4	20.4	9.6	10.0	6.5	11.7	6.0	4.1	2.0	13.0	5.1
1973	20.2	14.8	18.9	7.8	9.9	7.4	12.1	5.4	4.2	4.9	13.1	4.3
1974	20.0	15.0	18.6	7.2	11.0	7.4	12.3	5.7	5.1	2.9	16.3	4.5
1975	21.5	14.6	14.5	6.6	10.8	7.0	12.6	6.4	4.7	2.6	14.2	5.6
1976	21.2	14.1	19.0	9.9	11.9	7.0	12.6	5.9	5.5	3.3	16.0	5.6
1977	22.0	13.8	22.4	9.8	11.5	6.9	16.5	7.0	5.0	4.1	16.9	5.9
1978	22.0	13.4	28.1	9.3	11.1	8.2	13.3	7.3	5.0	4.1	17.4	6.0
1979	22.6	13.6	27.1	13.5	11.8	9.1	13.7	5.7	7.1	2.8	17.2	7.1
1980	22.3	13.1	19.7	6.5	12.8	7.4	14.4	7.1	7.1	3.4	18.3	6.6
1981	22.0	12.4	25.3	8.5	12.2	7.9	15.4	5.0	9.0	2.8	19.1	6.5
1982	22.7	12.5	33.7	9.6	13.0	8.5	16.3	6.7	7.6	4.6	20.7	7.5
1983	28.9	13.4	33.2	11.7	14.6	9.4	15.6	6.3	11.3	6.8	21.2	8.1
1984	27.6	13.3	26.4	11.7	15.2	9.6	18.4	5.6	9.3	4.6	21.9	7.2
1985	26.0	13.1	21.9	8.5	14.6	8.1	15.7	5.0	11.1	4.0	20.8	7.4

Suicide Rates

	Portugal		Scotland		Sweden		Switzerland		USA		W. Germany	
	m	f	m	f	m	f	m	f	m	f	m	f
1950	15.7	4.9	6.7	3.7	22.8	6.9	34.8	12.9	17.9	5.1	26.5	12.0
1951	15.4	5.3	7.2	3.7	24.9	7.5	30.9	11.8	16.3	4.7	27.4	11.9
1952	-	-	7.7	3.4	26.3	7.2	32.0	11.5	15.8	4.4	24.5	11.5
1953	-	-	7.7	3.5	28.2	9.0	34.1	10.1	16.0	4.3	25.7	11.7
1954	-	-	8.3	3.7	25.5	8.5	33.9	12.0	16.3	4.1	26.6	12.8
1955	15.0	3.7	9.6	5.9	27.2	8.5	31.4	12.4	16.0	4.6	26.0	13.0
1956	16.6	3.9	10.4	5.5	31.2	9.2	31.9	11.9	15.7	4.4	26.0	12.5
1957	12.7	3.7	10.6	5.9	31.2	8.6	32.1	10.4	15.5	4.3	25.2	12.5
1958	13.6	4.2	11.5	5.7	25.9	8.7	31.6	11.2	16.9	4.7	26.3	12.4
1959	15.1	3.6	11.1	6.1	27.2	9.0	30.1	9.4	16.7	4.7	25.7	12.6
1960	14.0	3.8	10.5	5.4	26.3	8.6	27.7	10.8	16.7	4.9	25.6	12.7
1961	14.1	4.3	10.4	5.6	25.6	8.3	25.9	10.9	16.2	4.9	25.1	13.0
1962	13.9	3.7	11.7	6.7	27.6	9.3	27.4	10.5	16.7	5.4	23.9	12.0
1963	15.5	4.0	11.2	6.1	27.1	9.9	24.9	9.6	16.7	5.8	26.3	13.1
1964	15.6	3.8	9.6	6.8	28.7	10.9	24.3	10.0	16.3	5.6	27.0	13.9
1965	14.9	3.7	9.3	6.8	27.7	10.1	27.5	9.7	16.4	6.1	26.8	13.8
1966	14.8	4.3	10.0	6.1	29.4	10.8	27.0	10.3	16.2	5.9	27.5	14.1
1967	15.6	4.1	9.9	5.3	31.9	11.4	26.5	9.1	15.7	6.1	29.5	13.9
1968	14.2	4.2	8.1	6.3	31.4	11.7	25.4	9.5	15.7	5.9	27.7	14.2
1969	12.9	3.8	8.6	5.4	31.2	12.7	25.3	9.8	16.1	6.3	27.7	14.7
1970	11.9	3.4	9.5	6.0	31.3	13.2	27.4	10.1	16.8	6.6	28.2	15.0
1971	13.8	3.1	8.8	5.8	28.5	12.3	26.2	11.4	16.7	6.8	27.6	14.9
1972	13.4	3.6	9.5	6.8	29.4	11.2	28.2	11.2	17.5	6.8	26.3	14.1
1973	13.5	4.2	10.1	6.8	29.5	12.1	27.4	10.6	17.7	6.5	27.4	14.7
1974	13.2	4.4	10.3	6.5	28.7	11.5	29.1	12.5	18.1	6.5	27.9	14.7
1975	13.4	4.2	9.0	7.4	27.7	11.2	32.5	12.9	18.9	6.8	27.8	14.6
1976	13.8	3.8	9.9	6.7	26.6	11.4	32.1	12.6	18.7	6.7	29.1	14.9
1977	13.8	4.5	9.8	6.5	28.3	11.2	34.0	14.3	20.1	6.8	30.2	15.8
1978	14.1	4.9	11.0	6.1	26.3	11.8	34.3	14.3	19.0	6.3	30.1	15.1
1979	15.0	4.8	11.7	7.5	28.3	12.9	34.5	15.4	18.9	6.1	29.0	14.6
1980	11.2	3.9	12.9	7.3	27.6	11.3	36.7	15.2	18.6	5.5	28.3	14.1
1981	11.4	4.7	13.6	6.6	24.6	10.6	33.6	14.4	18.7	5.8	29.6	14.4
1982	12.2	4.9	14.6	7.4	27.8	11.2	35.1	14.6	19.2	5.6	29.8	13.6
1983	14.7	5.2	13.8	6.0	27.3	10.9	36.9	14.1	19.2	5.4	29.0	14.3
1984	14.7	6.0	14.5	5.9	27.4	11.8	36.1	14.1	19.7	5.4	28.5	13.2
1985	14.1	5.5	15.6	6.9	25.0	11.5	35.4	15.2	19.9	5.1	29.4	12.7

Suicide Rates

	Yugoslavia	
	m	f
1950	14.7	5.9
1951	12.2	5.7
1952	14.6	6.2
1953	13.4	6.8
1954	14.5	7.3
1955	15.1	7.3
1956	14.2	6.9
1957	15.2	7.3
1958	14.4	7.6
1959	16.5	7.7
1960	16.5	7.6
1961	16.3	7.8
1962	18.4	7.9
1963	17.8	7.9
1964	17.6	7.5
1965	17.4	7.6
1966	17.4	7.3
1967	17.8	7.9
1968	19.3	7.2
1969	20.3	7.6
1970	19.6	7.3
1971	19.5	8.2
1972	19.1	8.5
1973	18.9	7.8
1974	18.4	8.8
1975	19.5	7.6
1976	20.6	8.1
1977	20.4	8.9
1978	19.3	9.0
1979	19.7	8.6

1980	20.8	8.7
1981	22.4	9.2
1982	22.8	10.2
1983	25.4	10.4
1984	25.3	10.3
1985	24.4	9.9

SUICIDE RATES 1901-1949

(rates after 1950 can be found in Appendix A)

	Australia	Eng/ Wales	Finland	Ireland	Italy	Netherlands
1901	11.9	9.6	6.1	2.9	6.2	5.8
1902	11.7	9.9	5.6	3.3	6.1	6.0
1903	13.2	10.5	5.3	3.3	5.9	6.4
1904	12.6	9.9	5.5	3.4	6.5	6.8
1905	13.0	10.4	5.9	3.6	7.2	7.1
1906	12.3	10.0	6.5	3.3	7.0	6.6
1907	11.2	10.2	7.2	3.4	7.3	6.8
1908	11.9	10.8	7.9	3.4	8.0	6.9
1909	11.6	10.1	9.3	3.3	8.7	7.1
1910	11.8	10.0	8.7	3.6	8.4	6.2
1911	12.1	9.9	9.2	3.4	7.9	6.2
1912	13.6	9.9	9.9	3.8	8.5	6.0
1913	13.4	9.6	12.5	3.5	8.8	6.8
1914	13.0	10.1	10.8	2.7	8.9	6.0
1915	13.2	8.4	8.9	3.1	8.5	6.1
1916	11.7	8.2	7.3	2.5	6.9	5.7
1917	10.2	7.3	8.3	2.2	6.9	6.2

1918	9.9	8.1	13.3	2.5	7.5	7.1
1919	10.5	9.4	8.3	2.9	7.3	7.4
1920	11.9	9.2	10.6	2.1	7.3	7.3
1921	11.4	9.9	12.0	3.1	7.8	6.4
1922	9.6	10.2	11.2	2.2	8.3	6.2
1923	10.7	10.3	9.3	2.5	8.7	6.0
1924	11.2	9.6	14.7	3.2	9.7	6.2
1925	12.1	10.5	16.1	2.9	9.4	6.2
1926	11.3	11.4	15.7	3.3	9.8	6.6
1927	12.0	12.6	18.2	3.2	10.6	7.3
1928	12.3	12.4	17.7	3.3	9.7	6.9
1929	12.3	12.6	19.7	3.8	9.0	6.5
1930	14.6	12.7	23.1	2.8	9.6	8.1
1931	12.7	12.9	23.4	3.7	10.1	8.4
1932	11.5	14.3	22.2	3.7	9.8	9.0
1933	11.9	14.0	20.8	3.5	8.9	8.1
1934	12.4	13.7	19.3	3.5	8.7	8.5
1935	11.8	12.8	17.2	3.1	7.7	8.0
1936	11.6	12.4	19.6	3.3	7.9	8.1
1937	10.5	12.6	19.6	2.9	7.6	8.0
1938	10.8	12.9	19.8	3.3	7.2	8.5
1939	11.2	12.2	22.7	2.7	6.9	7.8
1940	10.4	11.7	20.9	3.3	5.9	10.8
1941	8.8	9.9	18.2	3.0	5.3	6.5
1942	8.3	9.1	14.5	2.8	5.2	9.0
1943	7.1	9.1	17.9	2.6	5.0	8.1
1944	7.4	8.9	16.0	2.6	4.0	6.5
1945	7.7	9.2	17.0	2.4	4.8	9.4
1946	9.8	10.5	17.1	2.7	5.3	7.8
1947	9.8	10.5	16.1	2.4	5.8	6.6
1948	9.6	11.0	16.3	2.3	6.3	6.6
1949	9.8	10.8	17.2	2.6	6.6	6.2

	N Zealand	Norway	Scotland	Spain	Sweden	Switzerland
1901	10.2	6.2	5.3	2.0	13.1	22.4
1902	10.1	6.6	5.7	2.4	14.9	22.7
1903	12.8	6.7	6.0	2.0	13.3	22.7
1904	11.8	6.9	6.4	2.0	14.1	24.5
1905	10.2	6.1	6.6	2.3	15.3	22.5
1906	9.3	5.2	5.6	3.0	14.5	20.6
1907	11.1	5.8	5.9	2.6	15.5	23.0
1908	10.9	5.7	5.3	3.2	15.6	22.5
1909	12.1	6.0	5.2	3.5	16.8	22.6
1910	10.1	6.3	6.1	4.5	17.8	22.7
1911	12.2	5.6	5.3	4.5	17.6	23.7
1912	11.9	6.6	5.9	4.6	18.3	23.3
1913	13.8	6.4	5.9	5.5	17.9	24.7
1914	12.6	5.1	5.5	5.9	15.9	24.3
1915	10.3	5.9	5.0	6.2	15.4	21.5
1916	13.4	4.6	4.6	6.1	13.2	20.4
1917	11.3	4.6	4.3	6.0	10.2	18.0
1918	10.2	3.8	3.9	6.6	10.0	19.7
1919	12.2	5.3	4.9	5.2	13.6	20.5
1920	11.2	5.0	4.9	5.1	14.7	22.6
1921	12.8	6.6	5.6	5.2	15.3	22.8
1922	13.1	6.2	5.6	5.1	14.4	23.9
1923	10.4	6.5	6.7	5.7	14.2	23.5
1924	12.3	6.1	7.4	6.2	14.5	23.6
1925	13.0	5.8	7.6	5.8	13.5	21.9
1926	11.3	6.3	8.7	6.4	14.8	26.1
1927	14.5	5.8	10.4	4.3	15.1	24.6
1928	14.5	6.6	9.8	5.7	14.0	25.7
1929	15.7	6.5	9.8	6.1	15.4	24.4
1930	13.6	7.2	10.3	5.7	15.8	26.1
1931	15.7	6.9	10.2	6.7	16.5	24.8
1932	16.5	6.5	10.2	6.7	17.7	29.7
1933	13.7	6.2	10.6	5.0	17.1	27.3

1934	12.3	6.9	10.8	4.7	15.3	26.5
1935	10.1	6.4	9.4	4.6	15.5	26.4
1936	10.0	6.3	10.0	5.7	16.7	27.8
1937	11.1	6.8	9.1	4.3	15.6	23.9
1938	12.4	6.9	9.2	4.5	15.8	24.5
1939	11.7	6.7	9.2	7.4	16.2	23.8
1940	10.9	7.1	7.9	6.1	17.1	23.6
1941	9.3	4.3	7.8	6.9	15.8	24.4
1942	10.9	5.0	7.3	6.1	14.3	23.2
1943	8.6	5.7	7.3	5.6	15.1	23.8
1944	10.0	5.6	6.8	5.4	13.1	25.6
1945	11.0	9.2	6.2	5.0	15.3	27.8
1946	10.0	6.1	6.1	5.5	15.5	26.0
1947	8.0	6.5	5.6	5.1	14.8	25.2
1948	10.5	6.9	6.6	6.2	14.5	22.6
1949	9.7	6.6	5.7	6.2	16.3	23.8

Appendix D

SUICIDE RATES BY AGE 1960-1990

	Males							Females						
	15-24	25-34	35-44	45-54	55-64	65-74	75+	15-24	25-34	35-44	45-54	55-64	65-74	75+
Australia														
1960	6.7	18.2	22.4	27.0	29.1	38.2	32.8	2.0	5.5	9.5	12.8	16.5	11.0	9.0
1961	8.9	16.7	25.6	35.8	37.1	38.7	25.4	3.2	8.6	9.8	11.6	17.2	13.8	4.5
1962	8.8	23.7	29.1	35.9	40.6	34.9	36.9	3.7	9.4	13.5	19.1	18.5	14.5	10.3
1963	12.6	27.3	30.3	40.3	39.3	40.9	42.2	3.6	12.1	17.8	24.0	24.4	16.4	9.8
1964	10.4	24.3	30.4	35.9	36.8	38.4	41.0	5.0	10.1	16.4	22.8	18.0	20.1	8.5
1965	10.6	23.2	30.2	36.6	34.0	42.9	31.2	6.4	13.5	16.5	21.3	23.9	19.0	10.2
1966	9.1	19.2	27.5	33.4	34.2	40.9	42.9	6.2	13.3	17.5	22.3	19.2	17.7	11.5
1967	10.6	24.9	31.3	31.7	36.6	41.7	42.2	5.0	12.9	17.3	23.8	24.4	21.8	11.1

Year														
1968	10.6	18.8	27.3	28.3	37.5	32.3	39.8	4.0	10.9	13.9	18.8	17.6	12.2	8.7
1969	10.8	21.4	29.2	28.2	26.0	36.4	37.8	3.9	9.1	13.7	17.5	14.5	12.9	8.4
1970	12.4	20.1	26.1	33.6	30.9	31.2	38.5	4.7	7.8	11.8	14.6	17.0	14.4	9.5
1971	15.9	21.0	25.7	34.9	29.1	34.0	39.6	6.1	12.8	14.4	19.6	16.2	15.4	6.9
1972	14.3	19.1	26.7	30.8	27.3	30.6	39.0	5.8	8.7	15.6	18.6	14.9	10.8	8.8
1973	14.7	15.9	25.5	28.3	26.2	32.2	31.0	6.4	8.1	11.7	15.2	15.1	12.1	5.9
1974	15.9	16.7	22.6	29.6	25.4	32.5	35.9	4.5	8.4	12.6	14.2	15.1	12.7	9.0
1975	13.7	19.9	22.3	24.0	23.4	29.5	32.4	3.9	7.8	12.5	15.1	13.2	10.3	6.8
1976	15.0	20.7	23.9	25.5	21.9	31.1	27.1	4.0	5.9	7.4	14.0	12.3	8.1	6.3
1977	15.6	19.9	23.0	29.9	20.5	29.9	24.5	4.3	6.5	10.4	12.4	12.9	8.3	7.2
1978	17.5	21.5	22.1	23.5	23.3	22.2	27.8	5.1	7.4	10.0	13.1	12.0	10.4	6.7
1979	18.1	23.3	23.2	27.0	23.5	22.8	19.2	5.7	7.6	9.2	12.8	12.6	10.9	4.8
1980	17.6	22.9	23.4	22.3	24.0	22.4	31.9	4.5	6.9	9.8	9.2	7.9	7.1	9.1
1981	18.0	21.8	23.5	24.8	24.5	26.7	31.5	4.4	5.8	8.5	11.4	9.0	8.2	6.3
1982	19.3	24.8	20.2	21.8	24.5	28.0	39.8	3.3	7.1	8.3	12.6	11.1	10.3	7.6
1983	18.5	24.1	19.4	21.3	24.6	29.5	39.3	3.4	6.4	7.0	9.6	10.6	8.6	8.2
1984	18.8	23.9	20.1	22.7	24.3	24.7	30.4	4.4	6.5	6.7	10.6	8.2	6.5	5.7
1985	24.0	26.6	22.5	21.5	22.0	24.8	27.4	4.9	4.7	6.1	8.7	8.3	7.6	9.7
1986	21.2	28.3	23.5	23.1	24.6	27.1	36.8	5.4	6.3	7.5	10.8	8.3	7.6	6.2
1987	24.4	28.8	27.9	27.7	29.7	28.7	45.3	6.0	6.1	7.5	8.6	8.7	9.4	7.4
1988	27.8	28.2	26.0	24.4	23.8	27.7	39.8	4.5	7.2	7.5	8.2	8.7	7.4	10.0
1989	25.2	29.0	21.8	22.3	22.8	27.2	34.1	3.8	6.3	6.1	6.4	8.6	10.0	6.9
1990	26.6	29.5	26.2	22.6	26.1	25.0	31.4	4.7	7.8	5.6	7.3	6.6	8.1	7.9

Austria

	Males							Females						
	15-24	25-34	35-44	45-54	55-64	65-74	75+	15-24	25-34	35-44	45-54	55-64	65-74	75+
1960	17.6	32.3	36.6	56.0	58.0	60.8	79.6	8.1	13.9	15.0	23.5	23.2	27.7	22.0
1961	19.5	31.0	34.4	58.8	57.6	47.9	71.8	7.1	11.3	15.3	22.3	20.5	24.7	24.8
1962	19.3	33.7	36.7	56.3	60.6	60.1	82.4	5.4	11.9	14.7	21.6	19.4	24.3	27.3
1963	22.5	29.8	35.0	53.7	60.0	50.1	68.5	7.3	11.6	17.2	20.3	19.1	22.5	28.1
1964	21.6	30.4	37.6	63.6	65.8	56.7	64.3	6.4	6.4	13.9	24.5	23.0	27.9	26.8
1965	18.7	29.5	41.7	53.9	66.1	53.8	70.3	4.9	9.3	16.6	27.4	24.2	25.0	32.9
1966	21.9	33.6	42.7	47.9	66.1	56.2	75.3	5.6	9.2	15.8	22.0	23.8	33.8	26.6
1967	8.6	31.6	42.6	48.3	62.8	68.5	76.5	5.1	7.0	12.9	23.0	23.9	26.2	31.0
1968	20.3	31.0	43.9	52.7	60.7	66.9	62.4	5.4	8.1	12.9	21.6	23.0	25.0	23.7
1969	18.3	29.4	43.7	51.6	56.3	63.1	76.2	6.3	8.9	14.9	26.4	21.7	28.1	31.9
1970	27.0	31.7	46.6	58.5	64.6	72.7	77.7	5.7	8.2	16.4	22.3	25.7	27.6	29.4
1971	22.7	28.8	40.3	52.3	52.8	68.5	81.7	7.4	8.4	16.4	22.4	21.5	29.4	39.0
1972	20.8	29.6	43.6	51.0	68.7	65.0	88.4	7.0	10.1	12.6	22.6	26.3	27.4	32.8
1973	18.7	29.0	39.1	52.0	63.5	62.7	84.7	5.2	8.3	13.3	23.3	23.7	24.8	33.1
1974	20.1	32.8	45.3	59.3	56.4	66.3	87.3	7.2	9.3	16.1	19.0	27.5	26.4	35.7
1975	23.6	34.6	43.3	56.9	59.6	75.9	93.5	7.3	12.1	12.5	16.5	24.1	26.1	35.2
1976	23.9	30.2	41.4	56.9	51.3	65.8	80.7	4.8	11.2	9.9	19.1	24.3	26.7	32.8

1977	28.9	31.7	41.4	52.0	46.0	71.8	102.7	8.4	11.9	14.4	22.6	24.6	26.0	32.6
1978	31.4	34.5	47.2	56.8	53.0	57.6	99.8	9.1	10.7	13.3	19.1	24.5	27.1	28.3
1979	32.4	32.9	44.2	59.3	49.2	70.7	87.7	6.3	11.3	16.8	21.8	24.3	24.4	32.4
1980	28.8	36.3	43.9	59.3	56.3	72.6	85.7	6.7	11.1	14.3	20.7	23.0	29.1	33.9
1981	30.1	35.4	51.4	64.4	58.6	77.5	99.9	10.5	10.3	17.9	21.3	18.5	27.2	32.1
1982	33.6	46.3	52.7	66.4	52.9	63.7	110.6	6.8	10.2	16.5	21.1	21.5	27.1	29.5
1983	28.2	36.8	53.8	63.6	51.3	75.7	99.3	8.4	9.1	16.0	23.1	22.0	30.1	34.0
1984	32.1	37.7	51.4	57.0	53.7	67.1	111.8	7.9	9.9	14.1	21.3	21.3	26.3	35.9
1985	31.9	42.5	53.6	56.3	53.9	71.9	95.3	7.9	10.2	20.5	19.1	22.4	31.0	32.2
1986	31.0	48.6	53.3	54.2	52.5	72.8	106.5	9.7	14.3	18.5	20.2	18.9	29.0	31.5
1987	29.3	42.9	44.8	54.9	48.5	68.1	125.2	8.1	10.7	15.9	16.8	22.9	33.8	35.4
1988	27.2	38.6	42.2	48.1	47.6	58.6	107.5	4.7	10.3	13.6	16.5	22.5	22.9	29.7
1989	27.1	35.6	38.2	45.1	52.4	71.6	96.0	8.3	10.6	13.2	19.0	20.0	25.2	36.2
1990	25.0	32.7	37.3	47.7	44.0	66.8	107.6	5.5	8.4	13.9	16.5	20.8	22.0	35.5

	males							Females						
	15-24	25-34	35-44	45-54	55-64	65-74	75+	15-24	25-34	35-44	45-54	55-64	65-74	75+
Belgium														
1960	8.9	10.8	13.7	32.7	47.7	55.3	89.1	3.8	4.4	5.8	12.1	16.5	17.1	21.9
1961	7.8	11.6	17.5	29.1	49.5	56.1	93.5	3.2	7.5	6.1	13.3	15.0	15.1	16.8
1962	7.1	10.8	15.8	27.0	40.4	56.8	91.0	2.6	5.1	5.6	11.8	14.4	18.9	16.8
1963	6.7	10.5	16.1	29.3	43.9	46.6	84.1	2.9	5.8	7.1	13.9	18.5	17.8	21.5
1964	7.8	13.4	20.0	27.0	42.2	51.0	79.4	2.5	4.5	7.6	13.6	17.1	17.0	19.9
1965	9.1	13.7	17.3	28.3	43.9	51.2	87.9	3.9	6.9	8.9	14.1	16.9	22.2	24.6
1966	7.0	11.5	16.0	30.5	40.7	61.2	82.5	3.7	5.4	7.6	13.7	13.1	23.3	23.2
1967	7.2	13.8	20.0	29.8	41.8	52.4	93.5	2.3	6.4	9.1	13.0	17.9	23.2	22.0
1968	8.1	12.8	17.1	31.3	47.2	54.0	86.4	3.2	7.0	8.8	14.0	21.4	25.7	17.8
1969	6.9	13.6	19.8	26.4	48.0	56.0	93.4	2.3	6.1	7.2	12.3	20.6	24.6	19.3
1970	7.2	13.4	20.8	30.6	46.3	59.8	88.8	2.6	6.6	12.0	16.6	23.1	27.3	24.3
1971	6.6	15.8	21.0	28.6	44.1	53.9	98.0	3.4	5.5	10.5	13.6	18.7	20.3	24.1
1972	10.4	14.1	20.9	27.6	36.5	65.5	83.4	4.6	7.2	10.8	13.6	20.6	22.8	19.3
1973	10.2	13.2	17.8	25.6	42.8	55.8	91.1	3.2	7.1	6.6	13.5	17.5	24.1	21.0
1974	10.9	15.4	24.6	25.9	36.7	58.3	83.8	3.7	7.8	10.6	16.7	19.4	19.4	21.7
1975	12.8	16.4	15.4	28.0	40.0	52.8	88.7	5.1	7.1	14.4	16.4	19.9	25.9	23.4
1976	11.4	17.4	20.7	29.2	39.1	54.6	88.0	3.8	9.0	12.4	20.0	19.8	25.6	16.9
1977	14.8	21.8	26.4	31.4	44.7	58.6	81.6	5.2	11.5	13.6	21.2	24.4	30.0	20.6

Year														
1978	13.2	25.7	29.8	35.5	49.2	60.9	89.4	4.6	11.3	20.3	18.5	24.3	30.9	24.2
1979	13.4	23.6	31.9	39.7	47.0	63.8	92.2	4.9	11.4	17.0	24.2	25.3	30.2	30.1
1980	14.4	28.8	33.1	39.7	39.6	65.7	84.1	5.4	12.0	18.5	23.9	31.1	31.6	28.4
1981	15.1	28.5	34.0	42.0	39.9	57.0	98.3	5.0	13.7	16.4	21.2	24.3	28.8	27.2
1982	17.6	29.8	34.5	37.4	47.5	58.2	96.4	5.7	10.6	16.6	20.5	23.5	29.0	24.2
1983	14.3	35.8	37.6	36.7	44.2	60.2	87.1	4.8	12.3	20.5	27.3	26.3	27.4	26.9
1984	17.7	38.0	36.5	42.8	44.9	61.4	102.0	3.4	13.3	16.5	25.6	29.1	28.4	24.5
1985	14.1	31.6	38.5	42.0	48.4	56.2	101.5	4.4	10.5	18.8	22.7	23.2	32.0	29.0
1986	15.5	30.0	37.0	40.3	42.1	62.9	98.0	5.5	10.1	19.3	22.1	24.2	24.9	21.4
1987	16.0	34.6	36.9	41.4	43.5	56.6	103.4	4.8	13.2	14.4	21.4	20.3	25.0	26.8
1988	15.2	29.9	33.5	34.2	35.3	56.1	83.4	3.9	11.2	14.2	21.1	18.8	22.1	24.2
1989	17.3	26.7	35.8	30.0	33.8	46.3	99.6	3.9	9.3	13.3	17.7	17.1	21.8	20.8
1990	15.3	26.3	34.2	31.0	34.2	44.1	93.8	5.4	10.4	14.6	15.0	15.5	21.9	21.6

	Males							Females						
	15-24	25-34	35-44	45-54	55-64	65-74	75+	15-24	25-34	35-44	45-54	55-64	65-74	75+
Canada														
1960	8.3	15.3	16.5	24.2	29.4	25.8	26.3	1.7	4.1	3.9	6.6	7.7	6.9	4.0
1961	6.1	12.0	18.3	25.1	30.1	30.5	29.4	1.6	3.6	4.6	8.0	6.0	6.4	2.7
1962	7.7	12.8	16.0	25.3	29.1	19.0	22.4	1.9	4.5	5.1	7.1	6.3	4.8	3.3
1963	8.7	12.9	18.1	21.5	27.1	23.6	24.5	2.8	5.3	5.9	8.9	7.3	6.9	3.5
1964	8.1	15.6	18.6	25.7	30.7	22.6	23.9	2.6	5.7	5.7	9.4	8.8	6.8	2.7
1965	9.0	15.1	19.9	25.8	32.0	28.5	23.2	2.3	6.0	7.9	10.1	10.4	8.1	4.9
1966	10.1	15.0	19.1	25.9	28.9	24.5	25.9	2.1	5.6	7.6	10.6	11.7	5.3	2.8
1967	11.9	17.5	19.3	24.8	29.0	24.6	23.6	2.7	6.7	9.6	10.0	9.7	7.2	4.8
1968	11.7	19.0	21.6	26.1	33.3	26.3	20.4	3.2	6.5	11.2	11.3	8.8	8.2	5.0
1969	15.3	17.5	24.3	29.3	31.4	27.4	27.9	4.0	7.7	10.1	14.5	14.6	7.8	4.8
1970	15.6	20.1	26.6	27.9	31.9	28.0	24.6	4.8	8.6	10.6	14.5	11.4	9.5	4.6
1971	17.6	21.6	27.3	31.1	33.5	23.5	26.8	4.3	7.8	11.5	14.8	12.3	9.2	4.4
1972	20.7	22.5	25.3	30.3	27.4	24.7	23.5	5.0	10.3	13.2	12.6	11.3	9.1	6.4
1973	19.9	21.1	26.1	30.6	33.6	28.6	21.3	5.0	9.8	9.7	14.1	15.0	12.0	6.0
1974	24.1	23.2	27.1	29.4	25.5	30.5	23.6	4.9	9.5	12.1	14.7	12.8	10.0	4.2
1975	22.7	23.0	23.9	26.5	28.4	27.4	21.5	6.1	8.3	12.3	13.3	10.3	9.6	5.5
1976	22.5	25.7	24.1	29.4	25.1	21.4	23.7	6.2	9.6	11.5	12.4	12.6	8.6	5.3
1977	28.7	26.8	28.2	32.2	25.8	28.9	23.2	5.8	9.2	10.2	14.9	13.0	9.8	4.9

1978	27.8	32.0	27.9	30.7	29.5	27.0	31.9	5.7	9.1	11.5	12.6	13.2	10.3	6.2
1979	27.6	28.3	27.2	29.6	32.1	26.8	20.0	6.6	7.9	10.9	12.8	10.3	9.5	6.2
1980	24.8	29.5	25.1	30.7	28.5	26.9	38.1	5.4	8.1	8.8	13.7	12.1	9.5	5.9
1981	27.2	26.4	25.9	28.5	28.7	29.7	31.6	4.9	7.4	10.1	12.3	11.4	10.2	7.4
1982	25.5	31.5	27.3	31.2	31.0	30.7	26.4	4.6	8.3	10.7	10.9	11.0	8.5	4.6
1983	28.7	31.9	26.7	28.9	32.7	30.6	39.0	4.5	8.1	10.9	12.4	11.4	10.1	6.2
1984	26.9	27.8	25.3	28.6	28.8	25.2	33.0	4.3	7.0	9.2	10.5	10.7	8.4	5.8
1985	25.2	27.0	24.7	26.4	26.5	28.5	28.4	4.0	6.6	8.0	9.0	8.0	7.8	5.3
1986	26.9	32.0	28.5	28.1	27.6	28.4	36.3	5.3	7.5	8.9	11.4	8.9	9.2	5.5
1987	25.5	30.9	25.6	30.2	26.4	31.0	28.6	5.0	7.7	9.0	10.0	8.2	7.6	6.9
1988	26.9	29.2	26.1	24.2	28.0	26.2	30.6	4.9	7.1	9.8	9.9	6.9	6.1	6.2
1989	26.4	28.3	25.8	24.5	26.0	25.3	29.5	4.7	7.3	8.9	10.4	7.9	6.9	5.4
1990	24.6	29.6	26.7	23.4	22.6	20.7	32.4	5.0	6.4	9.0	7.4	5.4	5.9	4.2

	Males							Females						
	15-24	25-34	35-44	45-54	55-64	65-74	75+	15-24	25-34	35-44	45-54	55-64	65-74	75+
Denmark														
1960	12.1	32.1	33.5	50.8	53.4	44.8	56.0	4.2	12.6	19.4	25.1	24.7	23.6	27.5
1961	9.9	22.7	27.2	40.9	51.7	33.3	50.8	6.3	9.2	12.9	20.4	25.5	18.9	19.1
1962	10.6	27.7	33.5	39.6	48.4	51.1	55.2	7.2	13.1	14.6	26.4	24.8	21.3	20.6
1963	13.3	22.5	38.0	39.0	51.3	43.7	70.4	4.6	16.5	18.9	21.5	21.7	17.5	21.0
1964	13.1	25.5	33.9	52.1	43.8	51.8	69.4	6.0	13.3	19.3	31.3	29.6	22.9	27.1
1965	10.4	21.3	37.3	47.0	48.1	36.1	42.1	5.4	10.7	18.9	28.2	34.6	20.8	22.7
1966	8.5	24.7	26.9	43.7	48.2	44.7	52.3	6.9	9.6	16.2	21.8	27.6	20.4	11.0
1967	10.2	21.4	33.5	46.9	46.7	39.7	42.2	4.3	9.7	16.1	22.4	22.3	20.9	15.1
1968	11.4	24.2	40.3	46.1	55.3	44.3	53.2	5.4	13.7	17.3	29.5	29.2	22.4	25.0
1969	9.6	23.5	39.9	49.5	52.2	50.0	52.0	4.6	14.5	26.7	28.2	27.2	23.4	19.1
1970	11.1	25.4	39.5	55.9	48.8	45.7	55.0	5.7	10.6	22.6	30.2	34.1	26.7	19.1
1971	13.1	29.1	38.3	63.3	63.7	57.8	55.4	5.8	12.4	25.5	40.8	37.9	26.0	22.6
1972	12.9	21.5	45.4	58.0	62.2	53.0	55.3	6.7	12.8	22.4	36.2	38.3	29.2	21.6
1973	12.1	27.1	44.1	50.3	54.4	50.6	66.5	5.7	13.1	23.4	35.0	40.8	39.1	17.2
1974	17.1	29.9	42.8	59.8	63.8	64.6	70.9	5.8	10.3	19.6	37.0	38.3	37.1	33.9
1975	13.8	29.5	41.5	52.4	52.3	53.3	62.7	4.7	12.6	26.6	38.4	38.4	31.9	22.0
1976	14.4	26.8	48.5	49.6	57.5	53.0	51.1	3.6	14.1	18.6	34.4	42.3	30.0	26.0
1977	12.1	31.3	48.2	47.7	62.9	52.3	49.1	5.0	16.1	19.9	32.4	36.3	35.4	23.2

1978	12.2	26.9	38.0	46.7	54.5	39.1	71.5	6.0	16.1	24.2	36.3	34.6	33.8	25.4
1979	15.2	34.7	49.3	57.4	52.7	43.7	52.7	5.7	15.4	24.9	41.4	40.7	35.5	20.6
1980	16.3	42.7	61.8	70.7	71.8	60.4	81.3	7.7	16.7	35.8	42.8	39.3	32.9	31.6
1981	17.1	38.2	52.4	65.2	62.5	77.6	67.6	5.0	16.7	26.5	41.6	39.7	41.8	27.5
1982	21.1	41.5	45.5	71.3	57.4	47.5	69.1	6.8	17.5	26.9	40.5	39.8	34.6	27.8
1983	15.3	35.3	50.7	60.2	61.9	58.9	83.5	5.2	15.9	24.5	32.3	40.8	37.5	32.7
1984	16.1	37.7	53.2	57.1	65.5	48.8	67.3	4.1	12.9	28.3	41.1	38.1	37.7	32.2
1985	17.0	38.7	38.5	56.6	55.3	57.7	83.4	8.1	14.3	28.6	34.0	41.5	34.1	24.6
1986	16.5	33.2	50.6	54.3	62.2	52.9	65.5	5.2	14.0	24.6	36.7	44.2	29.3	26.0
1987	16.5	36.1	49.6	59.1	57.3	49.0	72.9	8.3	12.3	24.7	34.2	39.2	32.6	28.2
1988	15.9	33.6	44.7	50.5	52.6	47.2	69.2	5.5	12.0	20.6	33.2	33.2	36.0	33.1
1989	14.6	26.6	43.6	51.4	53.8	63.7	86.0	4.2	10.2	25.6	38.5	37.0	34.4	25.8
1990	14.1	26.7	44.5	53.0	43.7	47.3	76.7	4.0	6.9	18.4	27.3	31.5	30.0	32.2

Finland

	Males							Females						
	15-24	25-34	35-44	45-54	55-64	65-74	75+	15-24	25-34	35-44	45-54	55-64	65-74	75+
1960	19.3	41.8	54.9	69.1	72.5	57.2	48.2	3.9	12.1	14.0	18.1	17.1	16.1	6.1
1961	19.8	36.7	57.2	74.9	68.8	55.8	55.7	5.8	8.5	14.3	16.8	17.5	17.1	8.9
1962	22.2	45.9	55.8	69.0	81.7	64.7	34.3	6.8	12.3	18.2	17.6	19.5	11.9	1.4
1963	14.6	36.6	52.8	72.8	61.0	62.1	47.8	7.0	8.2	11.1	20.9	14.9	10.9	7.0
1964	18.7	31.1	45.6	60.2	72.7	69.4	71.4	6.3	8.8	16.5	21.9	11.7	17.2	9.6
1965	14.7	38.1	59.2	56.2	73.0	69.3	57.1	3.9	10.2	13.8	15.0	16.2	12.9	4.1
1966	13.9	33.9	48.9	62.9	64.7	67.2	42.9	5.9	10.5	12.5	18.6	15.1	19.3	4.0
1967	17.8	33.5	51.5	67.6	68.0	69.8	55.3	5.8	9.7	9.7	16.1	21.3	9.7	5.2
1968	22.4	42.9	50.9	70.2	68.2	58.5	70.1	6.6	11.6	17.2	19.6	14.6	11.2	3.9
1969	22.1	43.0	60.4	75.7	73.2	71.7	56.7	6.7	12.0	15.5	19.9	20.3	10.2	6.3
1970	22.5	41.5	55.8	60.9	62.6	66.5	50.5	6.7	9.4	11.2	20.6	15.9	12.2	7.4
1971	24.9	45.4	51.7	60.6	64.3	60.8	48.4	7.9	10.9	11.0	18.4	15.9	9.6	9.3
1972	30.0	46.0	57.7	65.6	71.0	65.1	65.7	8.6	12.4	12.1	15.5	17.5	15.5	7.8
1973	33.9	44.8	51.5	61.6	65.4	55.3	67.4	8.2	9.5	15.7	16.1	20.6	12.5	10.7
1974	37.3	47.8	67.2	63.7	60.8	58.9	47.4	9.1	12.4	12.4	19.9	15.6	14.1	8.1
1975	45.8	44.0	61.5	54.6	57.7	63.1	66.1	5.5	11.4	15.3	17.4	17.7	18.4	9.7
1976	41.7	53.5	58.7	63.3	55.8	67.4	61.4	8.9	12.7	14.9	17.1	12.3	16.1	9.7
1977	35.5	56.4	53.6	69.3	61.5	58.2	60.6	6.2	12.5	17.9	17.3	15.3	16.2	8.7

1978	35.7	47.9	62.2	71.8	55.0	55.2	87.3	5.0	10.7	16.1	16.4	13.7	14.5	9.1
1979	37.9	45.6	54.0	66.5	54.4	71.2	53.9	7.9	10.3	18.3	13.1	12.5	13.4	11.0
1980	37.5	55.7	55.0	60.3	54.9	62.1	60.1	9.1	9.5	11.4	16.8	16.2	22.8	9.7
1981	32.2	50.5	53.0	61.1	49.7	52.7	64.0	4.6	14.9	11.6	14.4	16.4	13.3	7.1
1982	29.9	54.7	51.9	57.8	46.5	51.0	61.0	5.4	10.4	15.9	15.2	19.2	18.1	8.8
1983	35.0	54.4	50.0	62.8	54.4	51.4	40.7	6.8	13.3	12.3	17.1	13.2	11.7	10.3
1984	37.5	53.3	56.8	58.0	50.0	55.7	70.9	4.7	11.5	12.1	17.0	17.3	13.5	12.9
1985	37.3	51.6	54.5	55.5	56.1	49.1	64.2	6.2	9.8	12.2	16.0	20.0	9.2	10.6
1986	35.1	51.7	57.3	74.2	49.7	55.8	72.4	8.9	12.8	12.7	19.9	13.6	20.1	10.2
1987	37.9	55.8	64.2	57.2	57.9	61.1	71.1	7.6	11.6	18.0	18.6	17.7	21.8	3.8
1988	39.6	60.4	65.8	64.4	54.7	60.3	65.6	7.5	7.7	13.2	25.4	18.3	16.9	14.4
1989	50.4	51.8	61.6	60.9	62.2	55.7	85.7	6.5	10.7	16.4	21.1	17.4	16.7	10.9
1990	50.9	64.1	68.1	63.7	56.3	49.6	90.1	11.0	12.9	17.7	17.4	19.8	16.6	10.2

France	Males							Females						
	15-24	25-34	35-44	45-54	55-64	65-74	75+	15-24	25-34	35-44	45-54	55-64	65-74	75+
1960	6.3	15.3	23.9	41.9	55.8	57.0	94.7	3.7	4.8	7.7	11.5	16.8	18.1	20.6
1961	6.9	15.7	24.9	42.5	59.4	56.6	91.4	3.8	5.0	7.0	12.7	14.5	17.5	16.8
1962	6.5	15.7	23.7	40.6	55.8	52.2	86.5	3.2	5.0	6.2	11.8	14.8	17.2	17.7
1963	6.6	17.3	24.0	41.2	55.9	56.7	88.5	3.9	5.9	6.4	12.3	14.2	18.4	17.0
1964	6.3	16.6	23.7	39.5	53.5	51.8	76.8	3.5	5.4	7.3	12.3	15.5	15.8	19.0
1965	6.2	16.2	26.3	40.6	55.4	51.4	77.8	3.6	6.3	7.6	9.6	15.1	15.2	16.9
1966	7.2	18.1	26.7	39.1	52.8	55.6	78.9	3.4	6.1	7.7	13.3	16.1	17.6	17.0
1967	7.6	16.8	25.1	41.5	54.7	54.9	77.1	3.8	6.9	7.7	11.1	16.0	16.1	18.4
1968	8.4	16.4	26.1	38.6	50.1	54.2	80.5	4.8	6.4	8.1	12.6	15.9	17.0	21.3
1969	8.6	17.0	26.1	37.8	50.5	60.0	79.1	4.3	6.5	8.4	10.7	17.0	17.2	21.1
1970	9.5	17.1	25.5	36.2	51.1	55.3	74.4	4.4	7.4	8.0	11.3	16.3	17.9	18.6
1971	9.7	16.4	25.2	36.1	47.3	56.0	76.9	3.9	6.6	8.9	13.0	16.7	18.5	19.4
1972	10.7	16.9	27.5	38.1	46.5	55.1	82.9	4.5	6.7	9.2	13.9	16.4	21.2	21.5
1973	11.0	17.1	25.1	35.4	45.3	55.9	83.0	4.3	6.7	7.7	12.5	17.6	19.4	19.1
1974	11.5	17.6	26.0	36.2	43.4	55.4	78.0	4.8	6.9	8.5	12.5	16.8	17.5	21.3
1975	12.0	18.0	26.6	36.3	39.5	55.0	80.1	5.0	7.4	9.0	11.5	16.9	19.8	19.3
1976	13.5	19.5	26.5	33.5	38.3	52.3	79.3	4.6	7.5	9.6	12.1	16.0	18.7	21.0
1977	13.9	21.5	26.7	35.0	38.5	49.4	77.7	5.2	8.6	11.1	13.7	16.9	20.8	20.4

1978	14.0	22.8	29.2	37.1	39.8	49.1	86.9	5.2	8.2	10.2	13.1	17.2	21.8	21.8
1979	14.8	28.1	30.6	38.8	43.6	56.5	87.3	4.9	8.7	11.8	13.6	19.0	22.5	22.8
1980	15.7	27.4	32.7	39.7	41.2	57.1	99.6	5.4	9.6	13.2	14.9	17.2	22.6	24.4
1981	14.6	29.1	32.6	40.6	43.8	58.5	97.9	5.0	10.1	12.4	14.5	17.7	22.5	24.8
1982	15.1	31.2	36.2	42.3	44.9	60.2	109.7	5.4	9.4	12.7	16.0	17.9	25.1	28.8
1983	16.5	32.7	36.8	42.9	47.6	64.0	112.5	4.8	10.8	12.7	16.2	21.0	24.8	28.7
1984	16.3	33.6	36.7	43.8	46.1	64.9	116.7	4.5	11.5	13.9	17.6	18.4	25.3	28.8
1985	17.0	35.2	36.5	45.4	48.0	61.4	120.5	4.7	10.6	14.6	17.7	20.8	26.8	27.5
1986	16.0	34.2	38.1	46.3	47.8	63.5	121.3	4.6	10.1	14.4	20.2	21.2	25.4	29.5
1987	14.7	32.5	38.5	44.3	43.9	54.9	113.4	4.1	9.8	14.2	19.4	19.3	23.5	28.9
1988	13.9	32.5	38.2	40.0	41.2	47.5	109.0	4.2	9.0	12.7	19.8	17.6	22.9	25.3
1989	15.8	32.2	37.4	39.2	38.9	52.9	107.2	4.6	9.2	13.0	17.4	19.4	20.2	25.7
1990	14.1	30.6	37.2	41.1	38.3	47.1	105.9	4.4	9.1	11.8	16.4	18.1	18.5	25.6

	Males							Females						
	15-24	25-34	35-44	45-54	55-64	65-74	75+	15-24	25-34	35-44	45-54	55-64	65-74	75+
Greece														
1960	3.2	5.1	4.1	9.4	9.6	17.6	15.4	6.4	2.9	2.2	2.6	4.0	2.0	3.6
1961	4.3	5.4	5.7	6.8	16.4	15.7	19.5	5.3	3.2	2.5	1.8	4.4	3.3	5.4
1962	3.4	5.2	4.2	6.8	7.4	10.6	16.7	4.4	2.6	2.4	3.8	3.3	2.0	5.3
1963	3.8	5.0	4.6	6.9	11.5	13.6	16.5	4.9	3.0	3.2	3.0	4.2	1.9	7.8
1964	3.6	4.9	5.2	7.1	10.9	9.5	13.7	2.9	1.2	2.0	0.8	5.1	1.9	3.8
1965	3.8	4.2	6.9	6.3	9.1	7.8	10.1	3.5	1.8	2.6	3.1	1.9	4.4	3.1
1966	3.2	3.7	3.5	9.4	5.9	8.0	16.6	3.2	1.7	2.7	4.7	3.2	2.1	3.0
1967	3.4	3.3	5.3	7.7	10.8	10.6	15.6	1.9	2.3	2.0	3.7	3.6	4.1	4.7
1968	3.9	4.1	5.5	9.5	10.9	12.6	18.9	1.6	2.3	1.6	3.3	3.3	3.0	5.8
1969	2.4	4.6	5.9	9.1	9.9	12.3	12.3	1.7	1.4	2.9	2.1	3.3	5.7	6.3
1970	1.7	3.9	6.1	6.7	10.6	10.7	11.6	1.4	1.7	1.0	3.2	4.3	1.7	5.6
1971	2.4	5.9	4.9	6.5	8.3	10.6	16.9	2.1	1.2	1.5	2.4	3.1	4.5	6.6
1972	2.1	3.9	2.9	5.0	8.4	11.9	13.7	1.4	0.7	1.2	1.7	3.5	3.6	4.4
1973	2.9	3.5	3.1	5.3	8.3	9.9	16.0	1.6	1.4	2.2	2.2	3.3	4.6	4.7
1974	3.4	4.9	5.4	5.7	4.9	13.6	13.6	1.7	2.8	2.1	1.9	3.8	7.2	5.0
1975	3.7	4.3	2.1	4.9	5.2	7.2	11.2	1.7	1.9	1.5	3.6	4.2	2.3	5.2
1976	1.7	3.3	3.5	6.7	6.0	7.1	17.4	3.0	1.7	1.7	1.2	2.5	3.0	4.2
1977	3.4	4.6	3.7	6.1	8.7	12.9	11.5	1.2	2.0	2.0	2.4	2.3	5.7	4.9

1978	3.1	5.4	3.8	4.3	8.0	6.8	16.0	1.8	1.1	1.4	1.5	3.9	1.5	5.5
1979	3.2	2.6	3.8	6.1	6.5	9.7	12.1	1.2	1.4	1.8	3.3	2.6	3.4	5.3
1980	3.0	5.4	5.6	5.2	5.4	10.1	16.6	0.6	1.1	1.9	2.8	2.9	4.5	6.1
1981	3.1	5.7	4.9	5.8	7.7	8.8	12.2	1.4	2.7	0.8	3.1	3.1	3.3	5.3
1982	2.9	4.7	6.6	4.8	10.3	11.3	13.1	2.4	2.4	1.3	2.7	3.0	4.0	4.1
1983	5.2	7.3	4.4	5.9	9.4	8.4	14.1	2.1	1.3	1.1	3.4	2.9	3.5	5.3
1984	4.5	6.6	5.8	6.4	10.1	10.2	15.5	2.1	3.1	1.6	3.3	2.7	4.2	1.9
1985	4.5	5.9	6.1	7.0	8.9	10.9	15.0	1.8	2.7	1.8	3.4	4.2	5.4	4.7
1986	5.6	7.6	4.0	6.0	8.1	12.1	19.5	1.8	1.5	1.9	2.3	3.7	2.6	5.2
1987	4.4	6.6	6.3	6.7	9.3	7.5	21.9	1.7	1.3	1.7	3.6	4.7	3.3	4.1
1988	4.8	7.4	5.7	5.9	9.9	7.5	17.5	0.6	1.6	1.5	2.9	3.3	6.9	6.0
1989	4.2	7.5	6.9	5.9	6.2	9.6	15.8	1.0	2.3	2.3	2.0	3.7	3.7	4.1
1990	5.2	6.3	5.5	5.3	7.1	7.1	17.4	1.1	1.5	0.9	3.0	2.1	2.6	2.4

	Males							Females						
	15-24	25-34	35-44	45-54	55-64	65-74	75+	15-24	25-34	35-44	45-54	55-64	65-74	75+
Hungary														
1960	29.8	38.2	40.1	57.3	64.4	66.8	116.8	15.0	12.6	14.1	19.6	23.6	31.7	47.9
1961	33.4	38.9	41.9	54.5	53.9	74.7	133.1	12.8	9.6	16.5	22.8	26.9	32.7	45.2
1962	28.5	39.3	42.7	52.4	59.6	70.7	118.6	12.7	9.7	17.0	20.6	22.6	34.1	48.9
1963	30.7	40.0	46.1	57.4	56.2	67.9	139.1	14.0	13.6	16.6	26.1	28.9	33.9	39.2
1964	32.0	46.8	48.6	60.6	64.4	72.1	148.7	11.7	11.3	16.6	25.2	28.3	38.9	56.8
1965	30.3	44.3	56.1	56.9	72.7	76.5	141.2	11.6	13.3	17.6	26.1	29.5	38.3	58.9
1966	28.6	41.7	53.1	68.3	70.9	70.5	137.6	12.7	12.0	17.4	28.5	26.2	38.9	56.7
1967	32.6	46.4	58.9	67.3	68.5	82.1	147.7	10.7	13.1	18.4	25.6	31.5	38.7	58.5
1968	34.1	45.0	68.5	75.1	80.0	84.1	147.7	9.0	12.5	17.3	21.5	35.4	47.1	70.3
1969	28.9	48.8	60.7	74.1	79.0	100.6	124.6	8.2	13.0	17.7	25.2	34.8	39.6	62.7
1970	27.8	48.6	63.6	78.4	85.1	104.9	146.4	9.6	11.0	17.5	23.8	33.8	46.2	76.4
1971	29.4	48.2	65.0	84.1	81.3	107.4	157.1	9.3	12.7	18.4	26.9	34.7	47.9	79.4
1972	26.3	47.7	72.3	89.2	89.9	99.0	151.0	8.1	12.5	22.3	32.6	34.6	47.5	64.6
1973	24.8	48.7	64.4	82.7	92.5	106.0	177.4	6.1	14.8	17.3	30.4	36.2	53.2	69.6
1974	29.3	52.8	68.4	97.6	99.2	122.2	174.0	10.9	11.4	21.4	29.8	45.6	49.9	78.8
1975	23.9	49.3	70.2	95.8	92.8	108.9	168.0	9.0	11.1	20.4	27.8	40.0	50.3	74.4
1976	25.6	49.3	74.1	92.9	94.4	126.4	181.3	7.6	12.0	21.8	32.9	42.0	59.1	82.6
1977	26.4	45.1	67.7	94.9	87.6	121.9	180.6	9.0	13.4	25.1	32.0	40.2	59.1	91.8
1978	29.3	52.0	72.5	100.2	103.9	119.5	184.5	9.9	16.1	22.2	37.2	40.3	66.4	86.5
1979	30.6	54.5	84.2	102.3	97.5	127.8	211.1	7.1	16.1	28.2	37.8	42.1	60.1	80.3
1980	31.5	58.3	86.8	106.4	96.7	116.3	202.2	8.0	16.4	26.7	36.2	42.2	52.9	90.6

1981	31.4	56.9	82.7	100.1	95.3	121.7	219.2	10.0	17.4	30.6	39.3	45.0	61.8	85.9
1982	26.0	55.2	85.0	100.8	91.8	123.0	209.7	8.8	13.1	28.5	32.6	42.0	66.1	74.7
1983	26.9	60.4	90.5	118.1	99.8	133.9	185.2	9.5	16.4	30.0	36.5	41.5	53.0	76.4
1984	26.7	60.6	102.0	111.9	105.7	113.7	196.0	7.2	16.8	29.8	30.6	37.2	55.1	85.6
1985	25.3	66.2	97.3	116.4	86.8	122.5	207.2	6.4	16.8	23.1	29.9	39.2	42.7	72.4
1986	20.2	66.9	95.8	112.0	99.7	113.1	188.7	8.5	19.2	29.0	34.1	33.3	52.7	80.9
1987	24.3	67.3	89.3	111.5	96.6	118.4	188.0	10.3	17.9	25.8	33.7	37.3	56.5	69.1
1988	21.0	57.8	79.4	99.7	84.8	96.0	172.9	10.1	19.0	27.2	34.8	35.9	46.8	74.9
1989	23.8	63.0	82.8	104.5	89.4	97.7	175.3	7.3	15.0	24.4	31.5	30.9	42.6	74.5
1990	20.1	56.0	79.5	99.6	90.2	97.3	196.6	8.2	11.8	20.3	29.9	28.8	37.1	75.6

	Males							Females						
	15-24	25-34	35-44	45-54	55-64	65-74	75+	15-24	25-34	35-44	45-54	55-64	65-74	75+
Israel														
1960	5.0	11.8	11.4	14.4	18.9	9.5	8.3	1.5	5.4	11.2	10.3	15.9	2.9	20.3
1961	3.5	12.9	10.2	13.5	25.2	27.3	0.0	5.9	6.9	6.6	13.0	11.1	10.9	6.1
1962	5.0	6.2	9.7	20.1	12.8	17.8	35.2	3.3	7.5	5.5	7.6	11.6	15.3	11.6
1963	3.4	9.1	10.1	15.1	26.2	16.8	26.1	1.8	4.4	8.2	11.6	12.1	33.7	21.9
1964	3.2	8.2	6.1	15.0	14.3	6.7	36.4	2.8	5.8	7.9	13.0	11.3	4.5	10.1
1965	5.9	7.3	12.1	14.8	14.4	24.6	11.0	2.1	3.6	4.9	9.6	18.0	28.6	14.0
1966	5.5	13.2	10.7	18.0	16.4	19.0	15.3	2.4	3.6	4.9	8.8	18.2	11.2	13.0
1967	3.0	10.2	11.5	16.3	23.7	25.3	34.3	4.1	0.7	5.5	14.3	15.3	5.4	12.7
1968	4.9	10.9	15.5	16.2	20.4	27.5	33.0	2.2	5.0	6.3	9.4	28.2	18.8	20.4
1969	5.5	9.9	12.4	12.9	22.4	16.3	22.4	3.7	6.3	4.9	13.2	15.7	19.6	7.9
1970	4.9	9.4	8.5	13.6	14.7	15.4	17.0	2.4	4.0	5.6	8.4	18.4	4.6	7.5
1971	4.1	9.4	9.8	10.2	14.0	27.3	32.0	2.7	7.6	4.2	6.7	22.9	19.1	17.7
1972	7.0	10.4	8.1	15.9	11.6	32.4	18.7	3.5	5.3	6.2	13.4	21.8	12.5	16.7
1973	7.3	4.3	6.4	10.2	19.2	22.8	14.1	1.9	2.7	4.7	9.5	18.4	23.4	25.3
1974	4.0	7.1	7.7	15.1	21.0	13.2	19.9	1.1	3.1	4.6	5.3	7.1	15.9	30.1
1975	9.8	8.8	15.8	12.1	16.9	29.5	23.9	4.8	9.3	7.2	12.3	15.7	14.5	23.1
1976	7.7	10.0	9.6	12.5	25.4	25.6	38.1	4.4	3.2	5.2	13.0	14.7	14.0	19.7
1977	7.4	11.2	14.4	14.5	21.2	13.8	17.0	4.7	4.5	5.2	5.8	13.1	15.3	12.6

1978	6.3	7.8	9.5	10.5	10.9	17.3	29.8	4.4	4.6	3.5	7.0	12.2	12.8	19.9
1979	8.3	7.7	15.7	18.9	19.2	15.9	23.8	4.3	4.4	4.0	6.4	8.4	17.3	18.8
1980	10.8	10.6	7.3	13.6	12.1	17.5	36.6	1.2	3.9	4.9	4.7	8.9	12.5	23.0
1981	5.2	9.7	8.1	10.2	13.4	22.3	19.2	3.6	3.5	3.2	5.8	5.3	18.2	15.2
1982	3.7	8.7	11.2	10.0	10.9	20.0	20.2	2.4	5.6	4.0	4.6	12.9	12.5	8.1
1983	3.7	11.5	10.6	9.9	17.7	23.9	44.6	2.7	5.1	3.3	4.0	8.0	12.8	17.8
1984	5.8	11.8	9.1	8.5	9.1	21.5	34.9	2.1	3.7	4.9	4.6	5.4	11.3	16.9
1985	5.2	8.3	8.2	13.3	14.0	26.4	36.0	2.0	3.4	5.1	4.0	6.0	14.5	13.2
1986	6.6	7.7	9.8	13.9	19.7	26.4	39.8	4.5	3.7	5.6	4.6	12.6	8.8	17.5
1987	6.7	10.2	8.4	13.8	20.5	26.3	43.8	1.9	4.0	3.0	4.6	6.5	10.4	21.6
1988	9.1	12.7	11.3	18.6	18.3	23.4	30.6	2.1	2.5	6.4	6.3	10.1	10.3	15.9
1989	6.2	13.2	13.5	13.5	29.5	27.0	58.1	3.6	5.2	3.7	2.2	9.0	14.1	27.0
1990	6.7	14.3	11.2	15.2	15.1	27.1	36.3	3.3	4.2	3.5	5.9	5.3	10.4	12.2

Japan

	Males							Females						
	15-24	25-34	35-44	45-54	55-64	65-74	75+	15-24	25-34	35-44	45-54	55-64	65-74	75+
1960	40.9	33.9	18.6	27.3	43.8	65.3	89.3	32.7	21.3	12.9	17.7	24.6	46.4	67.3
1961	34.2	29.3	17.0	23.2	41.0	62.7	93.8	28.4	20.6	13.1	15.4	22.7	45.2	68.1
1962	26.7	28.3	16.3	21.6	36.4	60.5	95.4	21.9	17.7	11.2	14.1	22.0	40.0	61.5
1963	20.6	25.7	16.9	22.8	37.2	52.1	87.5	17.4	15.5	10.7	13.3	20.2	39.4	62.8
1964	17.5	22.4	15.4	21.7	34.2	54.2	85.1	13.7	14.0	10.8	14.6	18.4	40.0	69.9
1965	15.3	20.9	15.6	22.2	37.0	55.0	86.3	11.7	13.6	9.7	13.1	19.4	40.1	68.3
1966	15.3	21.8	16.0	21.9	35.7	50.7	85.7	13.2	14.9	9.8	14.1	20.4	40.3	66.3
1967	13.6	20.3	15.0	18.6	33.0	50.7	77.6	11.7	13.4	9.3	12.7	19.1	36.3	65.5
1968	14.1	20.0	15.3	20.4	31.1	50.5	75.1	10.6	13.3	9.6	12.6	20.6	39.6	69.4
1969	13.6	19.8	16.5	18.8	31.4	49.4	77.3	10.8	13.2	10.6	13.3	19.7	39.4	69.0
1970	14.0	20.1	17.8	20.1	32.3	50.4	82.1	11.9	13.8	10.9	13.5	20.6	40.5	66.3
1971	15.9	21.5	18.7	21.1	31.3	48.7	74.0	12.2	14.0	10.3	13.2	21.0	40.1	66.2
1972	18.5	22.0	20.6	23.5	33.1	52.8	83.4	12.4	14.0	11.9	15.0	23.5	42.5	70.0
1973	19.9	22.4	22.9	21.7	33.6	53.5	87.4	13.1	13.7	11.8	15.7	23.3	44.9	73.7
1974	19.5	23.2	23.7	23.1	31.7	47.1	83.2	13.3	15.1	13.1	15.1	23.0	40.9	79.0
1975	19.7	25.3	25.9	26.6	33.3	46.1	84.8	12.2	14.6	12.9	15.0	20.8	40.9	72.7
1976	19.5	25.2	26.4	27.3	31.1	46.9	72.3	11.3	13.4	12.4	14.4	22.3	39.5	68.3
1977	19.2	26.0	27.4	30.4	31.3	45.2	78.0	10.0	13.2	12.7	15.1	20.4	39.3	62.5

1978	19.2	25.2	28.4	30.6	30.0	44.5	75.4	9.9	12.4	12.7	14.8	18.2	35.1	64.3
1979	19.8	26.2	28.8	32.5	30.5	41.0	77.0	9.8	12.2	12.7	15.2	19.5	34.7	62.9
1980	16.6	24.9	28.9	33.3	32.2	40.9	73.3	8.2	11.4	12.5	15.1	17.8	35.5	60.2
1981	14.7	23.3	28.6	35.3	32.8	40.6	66.5	6.3	11.2	11.9	14.5	17.8	31.6	54.8
1982	14.5	24.1	29.6	38.3	33.2	35.7	68.8	6.5	10.9	11.9	15.2	16.9	30.2	54.4
1983	16.1	28.3	36.8	53.7	43.1	44.7	82.2	7.1	11.0	12.3	16.4	19.7	30.2	59.0
1984	14.1	26.0	34.2	52.4	43.1	45.2	79.1	6.3	10.9	12.2	16.4	18.8	31.4	56.9
1985	13.0	23.4	30.5	49.6	41.4	42.6	74.8	5.9	9.8	11.9	17.3	18.6	29.7	54.3
1986	14.1	25.1	31.6	51.0	44.8	43.9	78.8	8.0	11.6	12.8	18.4	20.2	33.0	59.1
1987	11.6	23.7	29.4	45.5	40.5	42.1	73.0	6.5	9.9	10.9	16.9	21.2	31.1	53.2
1988	10.4	21.9	26.6	41.2	37.8	39.2	72.2	6.5	9.3	10.4	16.6	19.3	30.6	54.9
1989	9.7	19.9	23.8	33.2	33.7	38.7	68.0	5.3	9.4	10.5	14.8	18.2	29.4	51.6
1990	9.2	18.4	21.5	32.0	32.5	36.6	62.9	4.7	9.0	9.2	15.0	17.6	25.3	48.6

	Males							Females						
	15-24	25-34	35-44	45-54	55-64	65-74	75+	15-24	25-34	35-44	45-54	55-64	65-74	75+
Netherlands														
1960	2.8	5.9	9.8	14.4	21.2	22.8	36.6	1.7	3.7	4.5	11.2	11.6	15.9	13.1
1961	3.1	5.6	8.4	12.1	24.4	27.9	44.6	1.7	3.4	4.3	9.5	12.3	14.3	10.1
1962	3.7	6.2	7.1	11.5	18.0	25.8	45.6	1.5	3.7	6.2	9.7	13.7	15.7	11.7
1963	3.4	4.8	7.0	13.4	20.0	23.3	41.8	1.6	3.4	5.0	6.9	11.0	15.6	10.8
1964	4.4	7.3	6.0	14.3	17.4	23.9	42.4	1.9	3.9	5.0	10.7	10.6	11.9	13.2
1965	4.2	6.3	8.4	12.5	20.8	24.7	46.7	1.1	4.0	5.2	9.4	11.9	16.2	18.4
1966	3.8	7.7	7.9	17.1	20.2	26.9	35.3	1.2	4.9	4.6	11.0	11.8	15.3	13.1
1967	4.2	8.4	8.9	12.1	15.5	21.9	31.9	1.0	3.2	5.2	8.4	11.0	12.6	11.4
1968	4.7	5.4	8.2	12.1	19.8	19.4	38.8	1.3	4.2	6.3	8.0	9.2	12.5	13.3
1969	4.0	5.6	9.8	16.3	23.3	26.6	31.3	2.0	5.2	8.6	10.3	12.6	10.9	11.0
1970	5.8	6.4	11.1	15.7	24.0	25.4	42.5	2.1	5.5	7.5	11.0	12.6	14.9	17.5
1971	5.4	7.8	10.6	17.9	20.2	28.2	35.1	2.7	4.7	8.2	10.5	15.8	17.3	19.0
1972	6.3	7.8	11.9	14.4	21.8	24.0	45.6	2.2	5.6	9.1	12.5	12.6	16.2	12.3
1973	6.0	8.0	12.5	17.3	21.3	23.6	28.2	3.9	6.9	8.9	13.7	18.1	13.2	13.2
1974	7.8	8.6	13.4	18.0	22.2	27.2	36.1	2.6	7.5	10.8	11.2	15.9	17.1	14.3
1975	7.8	10.7	10.4	20.4	16.4	26.3	37.4	2.8	7.1	9.8	14.9	13.4	12.3	11.9
1976	7.1	11.1	16.5	18.2	22.2	25.1	42.8	3.2	7.4	9.2	11.8	13.6	13.8	14.7
1977	7.8	10.9	15.9	20.2	17.8	23.4	36.7	2.9	7.3	9.2	11.0	13.9	12.7	14.6

1978	8.1	10.7	15.0	15.7	18.9	25.5	30.7	3.1	8.4	11.8	11.9	18.9	16.4	13.0
1979	6.2	12.2	14.9	20.9	20.5	21.4	39.4	2.7	8.0	12.2	16.9	18.5	21.0	13.8
1980	8.3	14.9	15.1	17.1	22.3	26.1	41.1	3.7	8.0	8.9	12.4	14.1	14.3	12.0
1981	5.3	14.9	14.0	18.7	23.0	24.7	34.4	3.8	8.2	9.5	13.0	12.8	16.0	15.8
1982	6.8	13.7	14.9	20.4	24.0	26.6	39.1	4.4	9.2	8.7	13.0	15.5	15.9	17.1
1983	7.5	17.2	16.8	18.6	26.7	27.2	48.7	3.3	9.5	10.1	16.3	17.3	19.1	18.2
1984	7.0	18.6	19.0	22.5	23.7	28.6	42.7	3.7	10.1	11.1	14.8	17.3	21.2	14.6
1985	10.6	17.6	16.1	20.0	21.1	26.1	41.0	3.1	9.3	9.9	12.5	14.6	15.5	10.8
1986	8.1	15.2	15.3	19.6	22.6	25.5	42.8	3.6	9.1	10.9	13.6	13.5	12.5	13.0
1987	9.2	15.3	16.1	18.0	18.5	26.3	41.8	3.6	9.4	9.5	13.7	14.2	14.5	13.2
1988	8.2	16.1	14.3	17.2	20.0	21.2	41.3	2.4	8.3	9.3	11.2	14.0	13.1	10.7
1989	8.9	15.4	15.6	17.3	19.9	21.1	29.0	4.4	7.2	7.5	13.8	12.6	13.4	10.8
1990	8.2	15.8	16.2	14.8	16.1	15.4	34.0	3.6	7.2	8.7	10.1	12.1	9.4	14.9

	Males							Females						
	15-24	25-34	35-44	45-54	55-64	65-74	75+	15-24	25-34	35-44	45-54	55-64	5-74	75+
New Zealand														
1960	5.8	15.3	24.7	29.3	28.9	29.3	32.9	2.4	2.7	9.4	10.0	17.8	15.5	4.6
1961	8.6	15.4	21.0	19.9	27.4	36.6	26.3	1.2	4.1	4.0	10.6	8.3	15.3	4.4
1962	4.2	14.2	19.1	17.5	27.1	24.3	35.1	2.8	4.1	11.8	10.3	13.0	9.6	6.4
1963	9.5	11.5	19.3	25.4	25.3	36.3	20.5	2.1	3.4	7.1	20.4	21.4	14.9	12.6
1964	2.4	10.7	14.1	24.5	32.0	13.6	17.7	4.0	5.3	3.8	13.0	24.5	17.4	2.1
1965	5.9	11.2	15.7	32.2	27.7	26.6	38.7	3.8	7.2	7.0	11.4	17.5	11.8	14.2
1966	5.0	6.2	16.7	30.4	28.3	34.5	29.4	5.7	3.2	9.4	16.8	18.1	14.3	4.0
1967	9.2	15.7	25.9	24.5	33.6	23.8	35.9	2.7	3.7	7.0	12.4	15.8	23.0	11.7
1968	8.5	12.0	22.6	28.5	27.7	32.1	21.1	2.2	4.9	8.4	17.7	18.7	10.0	5.7
1969	9.2	16.0	17.9	20.7	28.9	34.2	42.8	6.0	7.2	7.1	15.6	15.7	19.6	3.8
1970	12.1	10.4	23.1	24.5	16.8	34.6	31.2	3.8	2.9	8.5	12.1	21.1	19.2	11.1
1971	9.5	6.7	19.4	22.0	19.9	21.1	24.5	4.9	6.8	5.2	16.0	16.0	10.6	5.4
1972	8.7	13.6	15.7	23.3	26.2	26.4	27.7	5.1	9.3	7.8	9.2	10.8	15.6	5.3
1973	10.1	13.3	13.1	28.2	22.1	26.0	39.9	4.7	4.0	3.3	13.1	13.9	11.0	10.6
1974	9.8	11.6	17.8	21.4	27.7	35.4	27.3	3.4	7.6	9.6	7.1	19.1	8.6	1.7
1975	13.0	11.6	20.6	20.6	26.7	23.5	35.7	5.5	6.9	9.4	11.0	15.8	11.5	6.8
1976	11.8	13.6	17.1	16.1	33.7	27.3	31.1	2.9	6.7	7.3	13.5	13.9	14.1	6.5
1977	20.4	22.9	22.3	28.4	20.8	21.6	47.4	4.0	9.8	12.7	9.2	16.5	13.2	8.0

1978	16.0	16.0	15.6	19.5	23.4	25.2	32.3	2.8	6.1	9.5	15.1	23.6	12.7	10.9
1979	12.2	18.5	16.0	29.1	22.4	20.3	33.9	3.9	6.0	7.0	8.0	13.3	14.4	10.6
1980	19.5	17.8	17.4	17.3	22.2	24.4	35.6	8.1	9.3	6.8	15.6	4.4	13.1	17.8
1981	16.9	15.4	22.8	20.1	27.0	31.8	29.3	3.5	6.6	4.4	8.2	10.0	8.2	14.1
1982	17.5	22.7	17.2	15.7	31.0	37.8	35.5	3.8	5.7	7.9	11.6	21.9	9.9	10.9
1983	19.2	19.4	19.8	15.6	22.4	34.5	32.0	4.1	6.4	11.5	10.2	10.5	11.6	9.2
1984	18.7	27.4	22.9	21.4	25.7	29.1	54.8	5.1	7.1	5.3	8.0	11.1	8.0	11.4
1985	19.6	20.0	14.0	21.8	18.3	36.4	38.4	5.1	5.0	5.6	6.6	10.4	9.6	4.9
1986	22.9	20.5	27.9	24.7	25.2	25.3	36.5	8.0	8.0	7.8	9.0	10.5	10.4	10.7
1987	31.2	29.9	22.4	25.9	29.4	23.2	55.0	6.9	8.9	4.5	11.3	7.7	6.0	10.4
1988	35.7	26.6	22.9	30.3	32.3	34.6	38.3	8.7	10.5	3.1	4.3	11.2	7.6	11.2
1989	37.9	29.0	23.2	25.5	18.2	31.7	39.2	7.0	7.9	4.8	8.5	9.2	9.4	2.2
1990	38.0	26.1	24.0	24.5	27.4	18.9	38.6	6.7	7.4	8.0	5.9	5.7	7.6	6.3

	Males							Females						
	15-24	25-34	35-44	45-54	55-64	65-74	75+	15-24	25-34	35-44	45-54	55-64	65-74	75+
Norway														
1960	6.3	12.2	15.0	18.1	21.8	13.2	11.4	0.9	2.8	1.2	7.2	6.0	3.0	1.2
1961	4.0	14.2	15.9	18.7	18.3	17.5	15.8	0.8	2.4	4.7	3.8	7.9	2.9	2.4
1962	6.0	14.4	17.2	20.6	28.2	21.2	14.0	0.4	3.0	4.4	4.2	8.8	6.3	2.3
1963	1.4	11.6	19.9	22.9	21.0	25.4	16.8	2.7	2.0	4.9	10.3	8.2	5.4	5.7
1964	4.5	11.7	9.7	27.3	23.3	17.0	21.1	2.5	2.0	2.9	6.6	7.2	4.6	7.9
1965	5.8	15.6	15.6	18.9	21.4	22.0	20.8	1.8	2.5	7.1	4.9	7.1	6.4	3.3
1966	6.6	8.8	16.9	17.4	22.1	14.8	17.4	1.8	1.5	4.8	9.2	5.6	6.9	2.2
1967	6.1	7.2	14.3	22.2	18.3	22.6	11.3	0.3	3.0	5.8	8.0	5.1	7.3	3.1
1968	8.0	10.3	22.2	22.8	19.5	19.3	9.7	2.0	2.0	5.9	6.8	9.6	4.7	8.9
1969	6.0	10.8	21.0	26.0	27.9	16.3	20.4	1.7	1.4	8.0	4.8	9.0	2.9	1.9
1970	5.4	15.0	17.4	19.2	24.7	19.6	13.3	2.0	4.5	10.1	10.4	8.9	6.9	1.9
1971	7.0	10.9	23.5	22.1	17.4	23.7	17.0	3.0	6.0	7.4	6.0	6.2	4.5	3.6
1972	9.9	11.5	16.1	24.8	24.6	22.7	14.1	5.1	5.3	8.0	8.1	7.9	6.7	5.3
1973	9.9	14.3	16.2	25.3	21.9	18.2	21.1	2.4	4.9	3.5	10.4	8.6	6.0	1.7
1974	14.1	14.8	25.6	31.3	28.3	20.0	19.5	4.4	3.7	5.1	11.7	6.0	6.0	4.1
1975	11.8	15.3	19.6	25.5	22.6	21.0	18.0	4.7	4.4	8.6	9.8	6.0	8.6	5.6
1976	12.4	17.2	24.0	24.9	25.9	28.5	23.6	5.7	5.3	7.1	10.1	12.2	6.3	3.1
1977	16.5	19.7	22.3	32.2	17.3	28.6	26.5	5.3	6.6	11.5	9.5	9.6	7.8	2.2

1978	18.1	20.9	20.3	27.5	27.4	26.9	20.3	6.3	6.1	11.2	11.1	9.6	6.2	2.9
1979	15.5	22.3	18.5	31.6	27.8	27.1	14.4	5.3	6.0	12.7	15.8	10.4	12.2	2.1
1980	20.4	18.2	20.6	28.6	31.8	25.5	24.0	3.3	9.0	6.7	14.2	12.1	9.6	4.7
1981	20.2	22.9	21.9	34.7	29.7	22.9	21.4	3.3	6.0	10.6	13.5	13.4	8.5	3.9
1982	19.1	21.2	29.5	34.7	33.5	27.4	21.1	4.9	8.0	13.3	14.2	12.7	8.9	4.5
1983	21.4	24.1	19.0	38.9	39.9	21.2	28.9	3.5	7.0	12.0	17.4	16.8	10.2	7.4
1984	25.4	23.4	24.0	27.4	36.8	37.4	21.2	5.1	5.3	8.6	12.8	15.3	12.1	6.0
1985	21.9	29.1	24.9	32.4	29.1	18.5	28.7	7.6	9.6	9.1	11.2	13.8	8.1	4.1
1986	20.5	27.0	25.8	29.7	29.3	22.8	18.5	3.8	4.9	12.0	16.8	12.4	13.6	5.8
1987	23.6	29.3	27.1	32.3	32.0	34.0	33.3	3.7	9.5	8.9	17.2	12.3	13.1	3.4
1988	26.6	31.4	27.5	36.8	34.4	25.4	33.7	6.5	11.7	13.8	14.3	13.1	13.0	7.7
1989	25.9	25.4	26.6	35.7	30.1	27.0	37.7	6.2	11.0	11.0	9.5	13.5	13.0	8.1
1990	22.1	28.0	29.7	28.3	34.1	34.3	30.9	6.3	6.1	10.3	14.1	12.8	13.9	7.9

	Males							Females						
	15-24	25-34	35-44	45-54	55-64	65-74	75+	15-24	25-34	35-44	45-54	55-64	65-74	75+
Portugal														
1960	8.0	6.8	13.7	30.8	37.9	44.5	72.8	4.9	2.6	5.1	6.3	6.0	7.6	8.5
1961	7.5	9.5	13.5	26.0	40.5	46.9	76.0	4.6	5.0	5.4	6.1	6.0	8.7	10.4
1962	6.0	11.9	16.6	23.7	39.6	45.0	62.6	5.1	3.9	3.5	4.3	8.1	7.5	5.8
1963	7.1	13.4	16.6	27.2	39.7	57.3	62.0	4.0	2.6	4.2	6.4	7.6	11.8	9.8
1964	7.6	9.6	17.7	27.4	45.0	57.1	54.1	3.0	3.8	3.2	5.1	8.4	8.9	12.0
1965	5.5	10.0	18.1	25.8	40.6	49.3	70.5	2.7	3.4	4.2	5.4	7.2	8.4	13.5
1966	5.2	10.7	18.8	26.0	39.2	45.8	70.7	3.9	4.1	5.3	5.6	6.6	14.9	8.1
1967	6.4	11.4	21.0	27.8	38.8	47.5	63.0	3.4	4.1	5.8	5.7	6.9	10.0	8.5
1968	7.2	8.2	14.8	22.4	39.1	46.4	73.0	4.0	3.0	5.3	6.0	5.9	11.8	11.1
1969	5.4	7.0	14.9	16.1	34.0	49.1	75.0	3.7	2.9	2.8	5.7	6.3	10.3	13.1
1970														
1971	3.7	8.1	14.5	23.3	36.3	52.2	80.4	1.4	2.7	2.9	6.3	5.9	6.4	10.8
1972	4.3	7.7	12.7	22.5	32.2	42.0	82.5	2.3	3.3	3.8	5.8	6.7	7.9	9.3
1973	4.4	8.2	16.4	23.0	31.6	43.2	61.6	2.6	3.8	3.2	5.7	8.7	10.2	12.8
1974	3.8	7.1	13.8	24.6	26.5	45.5	72.2	3.1	3.6	5.3	6.7	7.2	9.9	10.8
1975	5.2	9.2	16.6	23.6	33.3	37.0	53.8	3.4	2.6	4.2	6.2	7.6	8.8	14.1
1976	7.2	10.1	11.0	23.7	35.2	39.7	81.2	3.6	2.4	4.4	5.6	7.5	6.8	10.3
1977	6.8	9.4	16.2	28.2	31.0	32.2	71.6	5.1	2.4	4.5	6.8	7.1	10.1	12.8

1978	9.8	10.9	14.6	20.0	29.1	39.6	93.8	5.1	5.0	4.2	6.2	7.5	11.3	13.2
1979	9.0	13.2	18.5	22.5	27.8	43.6	83.6	4.1	4.5	6.6	5.7	6.4	11.5	11.1
1980	5.2	7.9	14.7	18.6	24.1	31.0	53.7	4.1	5.4	3.8	4.2	5.4	5.6	11.0
1981	6.5	9.2	11.4	18.5	21.2	25.2	61.9	5.1	3.3	4.0	5.6	8.1	10.7	8.4
1982	7.9	9.1	13.1	16.1	24.7	32.0	50.4	4.0	4.7	6.2	7.4	7.7	6.2	11.4
1983	9.3	15.3	15.1	20.7	30.1	32.3	47.5	5.2	4.8	5.6	7.2	6.2	13.0	7.7
1984	11.3	12.6	18.0	20.6	28.8	33.1	37.5	5.9	4.6	6.0	9.3	6.3	13.5	11.4
1985	9.3	12.3	12.4	20.9	24.8	38.0	54.6	4.8	4.3	4.2	8.3	6.9	13.9	13.4
1986	7.0	8.9	12.8	22.3	28.6	27.9	63.2	3.7	4.3	3.8	8.3	8.3	10.5	11.6
1987	9.1	12.0	15.9	17.8	22.8	33.1	65.9	2.8	4.4	5.3	5.9	7.7	7.8	13.7
1988	6.4	8.7	10.7	20.0	23.2	33.4	49.2	2.9	2.7	1.8	4.5	5.4	10.2	9.3
1989	6.6	10.2	7.2	11.9	21.2	28.8	48.0	2.1	1.8	3.3	4.0	7.3	7.5	11.7
1990	7.4	14.0	11.9	15.9	22.0	30.2	57.8	3.1	3.6	3.5	5.8	5.7	8.3	15.9

	Males							Females						
	15-24	25-34	35-44	45-54	55-64	65-74	75+	15-24	25-34	35-44	45-54	55-64	65-74	75+
Sweden														
1960	9.1	22.6	32.0	46.1	51.3	48.4	50.7	5.3	9.5	9.0	15.0	15.1	14.7	9.4
1961	10.2	22.9	25.5	48.5	49.0	45.7	53.9	5.3	8.5	8.7	15.0	13.7	14.1	9.7
1962	12.6	24.3	35.6	47.6	50.1	50.0	45.1	3.6	11.2	15.6	12.8	12.2	17.3	12.7
1963	12.2	23.6	30.9	53.0	45.9	47.3	48.4	6.9	12.8	13.1	18.8	14.3	11.4	7.0
1964	15.6	25.1	36.0	48.8	51.4	44.2	57.7	4.1	13.9	14.9	21.6	17.9	12.7	8.8
1965	10.9	27.0	36.3	47.7	44.4	50.5	54.1	5.2	11.8	14.8	16.7	17.6	13.0	8.1
1966	14.0	24.5	42.7	49.7	53.9	44.6	50.3	7.8	11.2	13.4	20.9	17.0	11.5	11.7
1967	16.6	33.5	43.5	55.6	53.3	47.2	48.8	7.2	13.1	15.2	20.8	16.8	14.4	12.3
1968	14.2	38.0	42.0	52.8	51.8	44.9	53.9	7.6	14.6	16.5	19.4	18.1	16.8	6.4
1969	15.5	30.6	43.0	57.2	49.6	45.6	56.1	8.3	12.7	18.1	23.0	21.3	14.3	13.4
1970	18.5	27.9	44.9	52.5	54.6	46.3	48.8	7.9	15.3	19.3	26.0	17.8	15.6	13.0
1971	18.8	27.6	40.5	45.7	51.2	35.1	45.8	7.0	13.0	17.5	19.6	22.4	17.1	9.2
1972	16.1	31.9	40.9	48.4	46.5	42.7	50.0	7.5	12.9	16.0	20.3	16.8	12.9	11.3
1973	20.3	30.7	43.4	45.1	46.7	41.2	47.2	9.5	9.7	15.4	19.3	23.1	17.9	10.9
1974	17.2	31.3	37.0	47.6	40.0	49.1	47.4	7.5	10.3	15.4	18.3	23.2	17.0	8.3
1975	22.0	26.0	37.7	45.4	40.7	38.9	51.9	9.5	12.7	13.3	17.1	18.9	13.9	10.9
1976	15.2	34.0	33.6	43.6	35.6	39.4	45.5	11.8	11.2	13.4	19.6	15.9	15.3	12.0
1977	17.6	31.8	39.9	42.5	37.2	46.6	45.9	7.5	9.4	13.6	19.5	17.0	17.0	16.1

1978	19.2	30.0	30.3	41.6	35.4	41.6	48.0	8.2	12.3	15.5	17.6	17.9	17.4	15.9
1979	16.6	31.4	38.4	45.2	39.6	40.1	55.3	8.5	15.0	17.6	21.9	17.7	19.1	12.8
1980	16.9	33.3	37.6	43.9	35.3	39.3	48.9	5.8	11.3	16.2	17.8	21.2	14.5	11.4
1981	14.3	25.0	29.4	45.9	34.8	40.3	37.9	4.1	10.5	12.8	19.1	16.1	17.6	13.8
1982	14.0	31.1	35.2	42.4	45.6	35.3	56.7	6.4	12.4	12.7	17.7	18.0	17.8	13.1
1983	16.1	31.4	32.2	44.6	35.1	41.4	53.8	6.2	11.6	14.5	19.1	15.9	15.1	11.8
1984	16.4	36.5	36.5	42.2	30.5	37.9	47.5	6.2	15.3	15.3	20.1	15.0	17.9	11.7
1985	14.3	32.0	29.0	39.3	32.7	36.2	45.3	7.6	13.2	15.5	14.8	13.8	20.1	14.0
1986	19.5	29.4	33.8	38.8	36.1	39.3	48.0	7.9	11.0	14.6	15.4	15.3	12.7	8.8
1987	16.9	30.0	30.2	41.9	29.7	39.4	50.2	5.6	10.3	14.8	20.1	13.1	12.6	18.3
1988	18.2	29.8	31.8	38.2	37.0	36.4	47.2	5.9	11.3	17.1	20.5	14.5	15.3	13.8
1989	19.8	33.7	31.0	35.4	36.0	34.6	53.3	8.3	12.6	11.4	12.5	16.2	16.8	13.5
1990	14.7	25.9	27.2	31.1	32.8	39.3	55.1	5.3	11.0	12.9	14.9	17.1	14.2	14.9

	Males							Females						
	15-24	25-34	35-44	45-54	55-64	65-74	75+	15-24	25-34	35-44	45-54	55-64	65-74	75+
Switzerland														
1960	24.5	27.0	30.5	40.7	52.8	56.5	62.8	7.3	10.9	11.2	18.9	21.4	15.2	17.7
1961	18.6	23.4	27.0	36.8	60.7	52.2	62.9	7.1	9.8	13.0	19.4	18.8	17.1	20.5
1962	20.8	25.5	33.0	46.8	49.5	55.5	52.8	7.4	8.4	15.0	16.3	16.7	17.9	21.1
1963	18.2	22.6	32.2	36.8	49.9	45.1	68.8	6.6	12.1	12.0	14.1	15.4	15.6	15.1
1964	20.3	21.7	30.6	35.3	48.8	47.8	48.6	5.5	9.4	13.6	14.3	16.8	19.0	22.7
1965	17.6	21.3	35.4	43.4	54.4	65.0	68.6	5.7	10.1	12.4	16.4	17.2	15.9	15.2
1966	18.1	27.6	32.1	48.3	48.1	55.5	57.6	6.3	8.8	14.5	14.6	17.9	22.0	17.7
1967	21.4	26.5	36.1	46.9	45.3	38.6	63.9	5.7	11.1	11.1	12.5	17.2	16.5	12.8
1968	18.8	21.4	31.2	46.3	48.6	48.5	57.4	5.1	7.6	13.0	17.4	16.5	19.6	14.4
1969	17.1	25.9	32.2	42.4	53.2	39.4	52.5	4.8	11.4	12.2	14.7	16.7	22.2	11.9
1970	21.3	27.6	31.2	46.2	49.0	49.5	74.1	4.7	10.2	8.8	19.5	19.1	21.7	16.0
1971	23.9	21.7	33.6	41.1	50.3	50.8	58.3	6.6	10.4	15.9	18.2	20.1	20.6	17.3
1972	24.0	25.1	37.5	38.9	51.1	56.4	69.5	6.5	11.2	13.0	20.3	19.5	15.5	24.1
1973	21.4	26.4	31.4	40.8	50.7	54.2	74.8	6.0	10.0	11.0	18.6	20.5	17.7	20.8
1974	24.2	27.6	31.7	44.1	52.7	54.8	84.4	7.1	11.8	17.3	17.5	21.4	25.7	17.7
1975	31.4	31.2	40.7	56.5	52.8	45.2	68.0	9.9	12.8	15.9	16.2	21.5	25.3	21.3
1976	28.8	35.9	38.0	46.9	51.1	50.5	73.3	6.6	14.4	16.6	19.2	18.7	24.4	16.7
1977	29.9	40.0	36.6	53.8	50.5	55.8	67.0	9.1	15.7	15.3	24.4	21.7	21.8	24.5

1978	32.6	38.0	36.6	48.1	54.8	52.1	79.4	11.3	12.3	18.0	22.0	21.9	27.4	16.8
1979	31.0	43.1	34.8	46.6	55.6	59.5	59.1	13.2	13.6	19.4	23.6	25.2	23.2	20.8
1980	34.2	36.5	42.2	46.1	63.4	58.9	80.7	12.3	14.8	17.6	21.7	20.8	26.8	23.2
1981	33.5	35.0	31.7	44.9	53.2	51.9	86.4	10.2	15.3	17.7	19.1	20.9	24.2	21.6
1982	38.5	42.2	34.3	41.2	50.4	54.5	71.4	7.5	15.3	17.7	21.1	24.3	26.9	17.6
1983	33.2	38.5	40.0	54.2	53.5	60.9	67.8	7.8	11.8	16.7	20.5	23.2	22.5	25.5
1984	34.1	40.1	40.8	43.7	50.0	58.9	66.3	7.9	13.4	16.7	21.1	21.5	24.9	18.6
1985	27.6	41.5	40.1	45.2	46.6	62.4	74.3	9.7	13.8	19.1	21.4	24.6	28.2	16.7
1986	29.4	36.1	38.2	37.8	47.6	46.5	79.3	8.5	14.2	13.7	18.4	20.4	21.7	19.6
1987	27.7	37.3	41.3	44.5	43.3	56.7	87.3	8.2	11.8	13.8	15.1	18.7	30.0	27.4
1988	26.3	38.0	36.6	39.6	41.7	48.5	74.8	7.1	10.0	13.7	17.5	19.7	22.2	26.4
1989	28.1	41.7	30.0	38.4	41.6	49.1	87.8	8.3	11.7	16.1	17.9	18.9	20.6	22.7
1990	24.8	33.2	32.2	39.0	42.7	51.6	86.8	6.3	10.9	12.8	19.6	16.3	23.1	23.5

USA	Males							Females						
	15-24	25-34	35-44	45-54	55-64	65-74	75+	15-24	25-34	35-44	45-54	55-64	65-74	75+
1960	8.1	14.7	21.1	31.5	37.9	40.4	55.5	2.2	5.5	7.7	10.1	10.1	8.5	8.6
1961	7.9	14.9	21.2	31.0	37.4	37.7	51.3	2.3	5.8	7.8	9.9	9.7	8.5	6.8
1962	8.5	15.9	21.6	30.9	38.0	38.8	54.3	2.9	6.8	8.8	11.5	10.4	8.2	7.3
1963	9.0	16.6	22.4	30.7	37.3	38.3	50.4	3.1	7.2	9.9	11.9	10.9	9.1	7.0
1964	9.2	16.9	21.2	29.9	36.0	37.0	49.4	2.8	6.9	10.1	11.6	10.2	9.8	6.0
1965	9.4	17.3	22.6	29.1	37.3	37.4	47.7	3.0	7.4	10.1	12.7	11.4	9.4	7.5
1966	9.7	17.3	21.6	28.5	36.2	36.8	49.3	3.1	7.6	10.4	12.0	10.8	9.3	6.6
1967	10.5	17.2	22.9	27.5	34.4	32.9	42.8	3.5	7.6	10.7	12.1	11.5	9.4	6.4
1968	10.9	17.1	22.0	27.2	34.0	34.5	43.1	3.4	7.2	10.7	12.4	10.8	7.7	6.0
1969	12.3	18.2	21.7	27.0	32.7	35.2	44.8	3.8	7.8	11.8	12.3	11.0	9.2	6.6
1970	13.5	19.6	22.2	27.8	32.9	36.5	41.8	4.2	8.6	12.1	12.5	11.4	9.3	6.7
1971	14.1	19.0	22.3	26.7	32.8	36.4	43.6	4.7	8.6	12.3	13.4	11.7	9.9	6.4
1972	15.7	20.9	22.2	28.0	31.5	35.9	45.9	4.7	8.8	11.6	12.4	12.4	8.5	7.1
1973	17.0	21.9	21.8	26.9	30.5	34.5	44.7	4.3	8.1	11.3	12.6	11.2	8.5	6.8
1974	17.1	23.3	22.9	26.6	30.2	32.9	43.8	4.6	8.4	11.1	13.0	10.3	8.0	6.2
1975	18.9	24.4	23.5	27.9	30.2	33.7	42.8	4.8	8.6	11.6	12.7	11.0	8.9	6.7
1976	18.5	23.6	22.8	26.2	29.8	33.9	43.6	4.8	8.4	10.2	12.7	11.1	8.4	6.9
1977	21.8	26.6	23.7	25.6	29.2	34.9	45.3	5.3	8.9	10.3	12.6	10.5	8.7	6.4

Year													
1978	20.0	25.5	21.9	23.4	27.5	33.1	47.8	4.7	8.1	10.1	11.2	9.7	7.9	6.8
1979	19.8	25.2	21.8	22.8	24.9	31.4	45.3	4.8	7.4	9.3	10.6	9.3	7.4	6.1
1980	20.2	24.8	22.3	23.0	24.4	30.2	43.5	4.3	7.0	8.4	9.4	8.4	6.5	5.4
1981	19.7	25.5	23.2	22.5	25.0	28.4	43.1	4.6	7.4	8.9	10.1	8.8	6.8	4.8
1982	19.8	25.3	22.5	24.2	26.2	31.2	46.1	4.2	7.0	8.5	9.5	8.8	6.9	5.3
1983	18.8	25.4	22.7	23.7	25.7	31.7	50.7	4.2	6.6	7.9	8.9	8.3	7.3	6.1
1984	20.5	24.9	22.6	23.7	27.2	33.5	49.1	4.4	6.1	7.7	9.2	8.5	7.3	6.0
1985	21.4	24.5	22.3	23.5	26.8	33.3	53.6	4.4	5.9	7.1	8.3	7.7	6.9	6.2
1986	21.7	25.5	23.0	24.4	26.7	35.5	56.0	4.4	5.9	7.6	8.8	8.4	7.3	6.8
1987	21.3	24.8	22.9	23.8	26.6	34.8	59.0	4.3	5.9	7.2	8.5	7.7	7.1	6.4
1988	21.9	25.0	22.9	21.7	25.0	33.0	57.8	4.2	5.7	6.9	7.9	7.2	6.8	6.4
1989	22.2	24.3	22.8	22.4	24.6	33.0	54.2	4.2	5.6	6.6	7.3	7.3	5.9	5.9
1990	22.0	24.8	23.9	23.2	25.7	32.2	57.9	3.9	5.6	6.8	6.9	7.3	6.7	6.0

	Males							Females						
	15-24	25-34	35-44	45-54	55-64	65-74	75+	15-24	25-34	35-44	45-54	55-64	65-74	75+
West Germany														
1960	18.4	24.4	27.5	42.9	48.2	46.0	55.1	7.1	9.6	13.8	21.8	23.2	20.2	19.6
1961	18.4	24.1	27.0	41.8	47.8	43.5	60.3	7.5	9.9	15.2	20.3	22.2	21.9	18.2
1962	19.3	23.2	24.9	37.3	44.7	42.5	61.5	6.2	9.1	12.2	20.5	23.5	20.8	17.1
1963	19.8	24.3	28.1	44.7	50.6	46.1	61.5	7.3	9.0	13.7	22.1	22.3	23.9	25.6
1964	20.5	24.6	30.0	46.8	51.3	46.4	64.3	6.7	9.6	15.4	22.7	25.5	23.9	23.9
1965	18.1	24.8	30.8	42.8	53.7	48.7	64.9	6.7	9.8	13.8	23.0	24.4	25.5	27.2
1966	17.5	25.9	32.3	46.4	55.3	47.9	63.7	5.0	10.3	15.9	24.0	24.0	25.9	26.7
1967	19.2	30.0	35.8	49.1	58.7	48.5	63.6	5.2	10.2	16.0	23.7	24.9	26.7	26.7
1968	17.8	27.4	34.6	45.3	52.8	48.5	65.6	6.0	10.3	15.6	22.6	25.0	24.4	25.1
1969	17.9	28.8	35.3	43.0	51.2	51.1	64.4	6.9	11.1	16.2	23.6	26.0	27.8	25.6
1970	19.6	27.0	35.1	43.2	51.6	53.9	75.2	6.9	11.5	15.9	25.4	27.2	26.7	26.6
1971	19.8	28.3	34.6	41.3	49.1	51.8	68.1	6.9	11.3	15.6	24.2	25.6	26.1	27.0
1972	20.4	26.1	34.1	41.3	43.1	48.7	62.6	6.3	10.5	14.5	22.1	26.3	27.3	28.7
1973	20.9	26.6	34.9	40.9	48.7	51.2	64.7	7.1	11.0	14.2	23.3	26.8	25.1	27.0
1974	20.4	28.8	34.2	41.9	47.6	49.0	73.7	7.4	11.5	14.2	23.2	26.7	27.0	28.0
1975	21.8	28.1	36.3	41.6	42.3	48.4	64.4	7.9	11.0	14.5	22.3	25.0	25.8	28.4
1976	21.7	31.7	37.0	43.3	43.9	48.9	66.9	8.8	10.9	14.9	21.9	26.0	26.5	27.2
1977	25.1	33.2	37.4	43.9	43.3	47.9	68.8	8.7	12.1	15.7	23.2	27.9	26.4	27.5

1978	23.8	33.4	36.2	42.5	41.2	50.7	69.5	9.6	11.5	15.5	20.5	24.9	26.6	26.5
1979	22.2	29.6	35.9	40.7	42.8	46.9	70.3	6.7	10.3	14.2	20.7	24.1	27.5	28.0
1980	19.0	26.9	33.0	42.0	38.9	54.0	72.8	5.6	9.9	14.0	20.4	23.6	27.1	25.9
1981	21.2	30.3	35.6	41.9	38.4	51.9	71.8	6.4	10.6	14.3	19.8	22.9	27.1	27.5
1982	20.9	30.7	36.0	43.1	37.9	47.7	75.3	6.2	9.9	13.7	20.0	21.4	23.1	25.9
1983	19.3	28.6	34.9	41.5	37.5	49.6	70.9	6.3	10.4	14.6	18.0	22.3	26.7	27.6
1984	19.4	27.9	32.5	38.7	38.7	48.2	76.0	5.2	9.0	13.6	16.6	19.8	24.4	27.9
1985	19.8	29.5	31.8	40.3	36.2	50.2	79.4	5.3	8.9	12.2	16.5	18.3	24.7	24.6
1986	17.7	25.3	28.5	35.6	36.7	44.7	72.8	5.3	9.1	10.5	14.8	16.5	23.6	24.8
1987	17.6	24.3	27.7	35.2	37.5	43.9	77.2	4.5	7.8	10.4	15.6	17.4	23.2	23.7
1988	15.8	22.7	24.4	33.0	35.5	41.3	77.8	4.7	7.7	9.5	13.6	14.6	19.5	24.1
1989	14.7	22.7	21.6	30.8	31.5	39.4	75.6	4.2	6.9	7.9	13.0	13.7	18.2	22.7
1990	15.0	21.3	22.2	28.2	31.0	34.6	72.2	4.5	6.9	7.6	11.4	12.8	17.1	23.7

INDEX

1979	10.1	16.2	25.7	37.9	45.6	63.9	5.6	4.3	8.5	14.0	17.6	26.9
1980	10.0	15.9	25.7	37.9	45.7	63.9	5.6	4.2	9.0	13.9	17.6	25.7
1981	11.9	17.5	26.9	37.6	47.1	71.4	6.2	5.8	7.7	13.0	18.2	27.5
1982	12.0	19.1	26.0	36.6	44.8	69.0	7.2	5.7	7.8	14.0	20.1	30.3
1983	12.1	19.4	27.6	40.2	41.9	69.9	5.6	5.7	8.5	14.3	21.8	26.6
1984	12.6	20.6	22.4	41.1	48.8	74.0	5.7	6.6	6.9	14.6	20.9	27.1
1985	12.0	19.9	25.8	38.5	42.4	72.9	6.0	5.1	8.2	14.3	19.3	25.3
1986	11.5	20.0	24.6	32.8	44.5	75.9	5.0	6.7	7.3	13.2	19.8	26.4
1987	12.1	19.1	25.8	37.0	51.2	76.4	5.7	6.5	8.7	14.3	21.4	32.2
1988	11.6	19.0	24.8	34.0	41.9	74.9	4.7	6.3	7.6	16.0	21.3	28.6
1989	11.5	18.9	25.8	34.2	46.5	74.3	4.8	6.9	7.0	14.3	18.2	29.7
1990	9.6	17.2	23.2	34.1	40.3	72.2	3.6	5.1	8.6	13.3	16.9	27.2

	Males						Females					
	15-24	25-34	35-44	45-54	55-64	65+	15-24	25-34	35-44	45-54	55-64	65+
Yugoslavia												
1960	10.8	13.3	22.6	39.5	38.9	56.9	11.2	7.7	7.8	10.1	12.4	19.1
1961	10.6	10.9	14.2	22.9	28.5	31.3	9.7	6.3	9.0	14.9	15.4	17.2
1962	11.6	11.5	13.8	26.6	31.4	34.0	11.1	6.9	8.3	12.8	15.6	17.4
1963	10.6	12.6	15.7	23.9	31.1	30.1	8.9	8.3	9.0	12.2	16.2	18.0
1964	9.0	11.7	14.6	23.5	31.1	33.0	8.4	6.0	8.1	13.8	13.8	19.3
1965	9.5	9.3	14.6	24.6	27.7	32.8	8.3	7.7	9.1	12.7	13.4	17.2
1966	9.9	11.0	15.4	20.1	29.2	32.3	8.3	5.5	7.7	9.8	15.2	19.4
1967	9.3	12.1	15.4	22.8	30.2	32.2	7.8	6.6	8.3	13.1	14.9	20.8
1968	9.2	11.5	15.6	23.3	31.2	34.0	7.8	6.4	6.5	12.2	13.7	17.7
1969	9.9	11.9	17.3	22.4	31.6	37.3	7.7	6.5	7.9	11.6	13.3	19.7
1970	8.4	11.8	16.3	23.4	30.2	38.2	6.3	7.0	8.4	12.1	13.8	18.0
1971	10.0	17.1	30.7	36.0	50.1	57.1	8.6	5.0	8.1	13.8	16.3	18.7
1972	11.4	17.6	22.4	35.2	48.9	55.1	7.2	6.6	8.4	14.6	17.4	20.3
1973	10.2	17.3	23.4	32.5	43.5	58.9	6.2	7.0	8.1	13.8	13.1	17.5
1974	10.1	16.5	23.5	31.1	27.7	65.5	12.8	4.8	6.9	12.7	19.9	22.3
1975	10.5	16.9	23.7	35.1	45.9	44.3	5.1	5.5	8.6	10.7	17.2	20.9
1976	11.3	17.2	26.4	37.3	47.7	57.9	7.1	6.3	7.4	12.1	18.1	22.7
1977	12.2	18.7	23.4	34.0	47.1	60.8	5.4	5.6	9.7	13.3	18.6	25.8
1978	9.3	15.6	22.2	35.6	39.6	45.6	6.0	6.3	9.2	15.3	15.0	27.5